CHRISTIANITY
AND
HUMANISM

CHRISTIANITY AND HUMANISM

Humanistic Traditions and the Christian Faith

By

Dale A. Jorgenson
Head, Division of Fine Arts
Northeast Missouri State University
Minister, Knox City Christian Church

College Press Publishing Company, Joplin, Missouri

Printed and bound in
United States of America
All Rights Reserved

Library of Congress Catalog Card Number: 83-70878
International Standard Book Number: 0-89900-149-1

To Mary Lee and to my mother, both of whom deserve a
much larger and more impressive book

vi

TABLE OF CONTENTS

Christians today must understand the spirit of the age. They must realize that the protesters and revolutionaries are often fighting against the same evils of society as they are themselves. But they must also see the inadequacy of all answers that do not tackle the root of the problem.

H. R. Rookmaaker
Modern Art and the Death of a Culture

x

INTRODUCTION

The five introductory essays in this little volume were first presented as lectures to members of the Woodland Bible Camp at Linton, Indiana during the summer of 1981. The audience for the series consisted largely of people who are conservative in theology, open in terms of fellowship, and who are heirs of the tradition of the "Restoration Movement" in the United States—that thrust for Christian unity which had its origins during the early nineteenth century through the ministries of Thomas and Alexander Campbell, Barton W. Stone, Walter Scott, and many other creative disciples. For this reason, some of the material in these essays relates to the thought and practice of the churches which have emerged from the "Campbell tradition": the Christian Churches (Disciples of Christ), the Christian Churches, and the Churches of Christ.

"Humanism" has become a familiar and somewhat tainted word among evangelical Christians in mid-century America. Newspaper articles describe the attempts of outraged parents to deal with the nontheistic bias presented their children in many public schools, Christian schools battle the courts because of the incursions of the Internal Revenue Service and state education departments into the fiscal operations and curricula of church-related schools, and most institutions of higher education seem to proceed on the assumption that Judeo-Christian beliefs are archaic and the relevance of theism is all history. While many scientists and thoughtful humanists have rejected the easy optimism of the *Humanist Manifesto* of 1933 or its update in 1973—a rejection mandated intellectually by events of the post-World War II period—other options proposed for serious consideration in academic circles tend to be equally nontheistic and to reject the Christian claim of a revealed religion and a living Christ.

But most "-isms" tend to become symbolic terms which invite rejection *en toto* and thus fail to receive the necessary analysis for discriminating debate. "So fight I, as not beating the air . . ." writes the Apostle Paul, and so should it be with Christians in dealing with the problems of naturalistic humanism. There is a familiar saying dealing with babies and bathwater, and it does seem incumbent upon serious Christian students of the current generation to attempt definition of just what it is they are against.

Realizing that a twenty-page summary of classic humanism reeks of the superficial, and a similar essay on Renaissance humanism attempts to project a definition in a few words of that which serious Renaissance scholars have not been able to do in thousands of pages, the writer submits this introductory series of essays with a full cognizance of their outline nature. In the same vein, the two-essay critique of twentieth-century naturalistic humanism together with critical references to some other current thought systems which compete for the Christian's attention is submitted as only an introduction. Certainly the last essay, projecting the author's basic views concerning a Christian image of man, is intended only to suggest an alternative to the nontheistic faith about the human race projected by contemporary and naturalistic humanism.

But the choice and order of subjects outlining the historic cornerstones of humanistic thought may be of some help to those struggling with this concept, and the author dares to hope that this presentation, together with the basic bibliography, will be of use to disciples of Jesus Christ who are trying to discriminate between that which opposes the cross of Christ and that which may be an instrument of that cross. These essays are therefore dedicated to God's greatest creation, Man, who finds himself not only the object of creation but of God's New Creation in Jesus Christ our Lord.

1

THE CLASSICAL IMAGE OF MAN

The Apostle Paul apparently found the university town of Athens a depressing place. Luke refers to the provocation of his spirit in these words: "Now while Paul was waiting for them (Silas and Timothy) at Athens, his spirit was provoked within him as he saw that the city was full of idols" (Acts 17:16, RSV).

But Paul's own words in the first letter to the Thessalonians, probably written a few months later at Corinth while he was remembering the Athenian visit, tell us more about his inner feelings:

> But since we were bereft of you, brethren, for a short time, in person not in heart, we endeavored the more eagerly and with great desire to see you face to face; because we wanted to come to you—I, Paul, again and again—but Satan hindered us. For what is our hope and joy or crown of boasting before our Lord Jesus at his coming? Is it not you? For you are our glory and joy.

Therefore when we could bear it no longer, we were willing to be left behind at Athens alone, and we sent Timothy, our brother and God's servant in the gospel of Christ, to establish you in your faith and to exhort you, that no one be moved by these afflictions. You yourselves know that this is to be our lot. For when we were with you, we told you beforehand that we were to suffer affliction; just as it has come to pass, and as you know (I Thess. 2:17—3:4).

Paul emphasizes his own Jewishness in the brief autobiographical statement he offers in Acts 26. However, growing up in Tarsus, a university city with a strong mixture of Hellenistic and Oriental culture, he could hardly have failed to imbibe at least a limited understanding of Greek philosophy and tradition. Elias Andrews points out, "Tarsus, with its hellenistic-oriental character, furnished Paul with a background which later proved invaluable as he ventured into the Roman world to proclaim the gospel of Christ." But he adds, "There is little evidence that Paul was trained in Greek culture or had firsthand knowledge of the mystery cults."[1]

So the Apostle can hardly be considered a partaker in classical humanism as we watch him enter the Areopagus by the gate which led from the Peraeus, a rocky crag which is elevated above the neighboring shore and, according to Coneybeare and Howson, was originally entirely insulated in the sea.[2] Karl Zimmerman, in his little book, *Der Apostel Paulus,* emphasizes the fact that Paul did not enter the center and source of European culture and the five-hundred year world-famous center of art and architecture with much concern for its artistic qualities. Paul entered the city with a single-minded and burning intention to install

---

1. Elias Andrews, "Paul" in *Encyclopaedia Britannica* (Chicago: William Benton, Publisher), 1963, p. 388.

2. Coneybeare and Howson, *The Life and Epistles of St. Paul* (Grand Rapids: Wm. B. Eerdmans Pub. Co., 1980), p. 273.

the religion of the cross. And in this, as Luke reports, he was not very successful.[3]

Coming into the city by the route we expect him to have taken, Paul probably witnessed sculptured forms of Minerva, Jupiter, Apollo, Mercury, the Muses, an entire sanctuary devoted to the worship of Bacchus, and statues of historical heroes who were deified by various generations of Greeks. These would have included Hercules, Theseus, Ceres, an altar of Vesta, and even statues of some of the leaders from the Roman world.[4] This incomparable art gallery which might gladden the heart of any twentieth-century curator, when perceived through Paul's eyes as the ultimate idolatry it represented, must have added to his feeling of spiritual illness and revulsion reported by Luke: "His spirit was stirred within him, when he saw the city crowded with idols."[5]

But Paul, in his perception of the city, could not have missed the philosophical trappings still remaining: the sources of the classic humanism we are discussing. Two memorable suburbs contained the sites of the Academy of Plato and the Lyceum of Aristotle. Luke mentions the two dominant schools of philosophy which were still active during the Roman occupation and Paul's visit: the Epicurean and the Stoic (Acts 17:18). And the sacred text also mentions (through the interpretation of the Christian doctor writing the text) the intense interest still maintained by the Greeks in what they would have called intellectual discourse, an activity dismissed by the chronicler of Acts with the words, "Now all the Athenians and the foreigners who lived there spent their time in nothing except telling or hearing something new" (Acts 17:21).

For our purposes, we will look very briefly at Greek humanism expressed by Homer, Plato, Aristotle, and finally the Stoics and Epicureans.

---

3. Karl Zimmerman, *Der Apostel Paulus, ein Lebensbild* (Zurich: Zwingli Verlag, 1962), pp. 71-72. See Acts 17:34.
4. Coneybeare and Howson, pp. 275-277.
5. Acts 17:16.

The Apostle Paul uses the expression, "the times of ignorance" referring to the very periods when classical culture gave the world the philosophical and artistic models for European civilization. However, as Stuart Barton Babbage writes in his excellent little book, *Man in Nature and in Grace,* "Nevertheless, the insights and intuitions of the ancient world are neither to be despised nor lightly dismissed."[6] The Greek thinkers dealt with the ultimate questions which are swept aside as being either unanswerable or irrelevant by many of today's philosophical systems. My uncle used to say that he felt Plato was very close to understanding the questions Jesus posed, and that had he lived at a time when he could have heard the teachings of the Christ he would have been a disciple. I have doubts about this judgment, but do believe that we are making a mistake when, as followers of Jesus, we discard the good things which have gone into the fabric of human history without an honest look. Jesus himself told His prospective disciples, "Come and see."[7] It is a fair challenge.

HUMANISM IN HOMER

Two strong poetic lays describing the ancient saga of Troy and the Greeks have come down to us in the *Iliad* and the *Odyssey.* The special theme of the *Iliad* is "a calamitous quarrel between the Achaean leaders before Troy and what came of it, the theme of the second the wanderings of King Odysseus after the fall of Troy before he came home to wife and son again. Their author, according to ancient tradition, was one Homer, who lived between 800 and 900 B.C. in one of the Ionian Greek communities on the eastern shore of the Aegean."[8]

6. Stuart Barton Babbage, *Man in Nature and in Grace* (Grand Rapids: Wm. B. Eerdmans Publishing Co., 1957), p. 24.

7. Jn. 1:39.

8. Louise R. Loomis, "Introduction" to *The Iliad of Homer,* tr. by Samuel Butler (New York: The Classics Club, Walter J. Black, Publisher, 1942), p. xviii.

During the nineteenth and early twentieth centuries numerous scholars developed a theory questioning the actual existence of Homer as an individual, suggesting that the *Iliad* and *Odyssey* were compilations of a number of separate poems from numerous folk traditions. More recent scholarship has generally restored the person of Homer to his poetry, suggesting that the *Iliad* was done in his youth and the *Odyssey* later in his life.[9]

The conception of man developed by Homer would seem to me to include the following traits:

1. The glorification of the human body, particularly the warrior's and athlete's body, as the joy of life. Babbage comments that in Homer, "Nothing is so desirable as a robust physical frame; it is a prerequisite for the strenuous activities of love and war."[10]

2. In common with later Greek thought, the Homeric view of *the good* depends upon a golden mean, a balance between extremes which is sometimes labeled *sophrosyne*. Sin is a breach of this balance.

3. Man is a union of two distinct kinds of being: the body and the soul. The Homeric conception of man "lacks the dimension of eternity."[11] While the soul is not overlooked, the body provides the vehicle through which greatness, joy, and human meaning are achieved.

4. Man is sometimes regarded with some melancholy if not despair. This may be related to the emphasis upon the ephemeral nature of man, and the mortality of man is one of the specific ways in which he differs sharply from the gods.

The origin of the Olympic Games about 776 B.C. is worth keeping in mind as one considers the Homeric ethos. The games were restricted to Greeks, only male competitors were allowed

---

9. Loomis, pp. xxv-xxvi.
10. Babbage, p. 24.
11. Babbage, p. 25.

to participate, kings and commoners competed together, and the oath of participation underlined the resolve to keep the competition clean and the decisions just. Although the Roman emperor Theodosius abolished the games in 394 A.D. after Greece lost its independence, the impact of the heroic personality of the Greek warrior or the athlete in the games had caught the imagination of the world sufficiently to effect the revival of the Olympics in 1896. It is well known that Hitler attempted to subvert the spirit of the games for his purposes in 1936 when the victorious black American, Jesse Owens, upset the Third Reich emphasis upon racial superiority and German nationalism.

A few references from Homer's work will illustrate some of the philosophical beliefs outlined above. In Book III of the *Iliad*, King Priam of Troy takes occasion to ask fair Helen about several of the Achaean warriors they see before them:

> "Tell me, then, who is yonder huge hero so great and goodly? I have seen men taller by a head, but none so comely and so royal. Surely he must be the king."
>
> "Sir," answered Helen . . . "As for your question, the hero of whom you ask is Agamemnon, son of Atreus, a good king and a brave soldier. . . ."
>
> . . . . .
>
> The old man next looked upon Odysseus. "Tell me," he said, "who is that other shorter by a head than Agamemnon, but broader across the chest and shoulders? His armor is laid upon the ground, and he stalks in front of the ranks as it were some great woolly ram ordering his ewes."
>
> And Helen answered: "He is Odysseus, a man of great craft, son of Laertes. He was born in rugged Ithaca, and excels in all manner of stratagems and subtle cunning."
>
> . . . . .

Priam then caught sight of Ajax and asked, "Who is that great and goodly warrior whose head and broad shoulders tower above the rest of the Argives?"

"That," answered Helen, "is huge Ajax, bulwark of the Achaeans, and on the other side of him, among the Cretans, stands Domeneus looking like a god, and with the captains of the Cretans round him."[12]

The external physical characteristics of a man are often alluded to in search of his character, and aging is considered a grievous calamity. King Priam of Troy is pictured in Book III as a beaten old man when his son, Paris, prepares to meet the Greek, Menelaus. Paris is the implied villain of most of the saga, since it was he who not only stole Helen, the wife of Menelaus, thus beginning the conflict, but who watched the entire Trojan kingdom come apart defending his dishonorable act. He participated in the battle he had caused only between taking good care of his appearance and enjoying his free time with Helen. But finally Menelaus succeeds in challenging him to single-handed combat.

Paris' tired old father can't manage to watch, as the *Iliad* reports the scene:

The old man trembled as he heard, but bade his followers yoke the horses, and they all made haste to do so.

. . . . .

Then Priam, descendant of Dardanus, spoke, saying, "Hear me, Trojans and Achaeans, I will now go back to the wind-beaten city of Ilium. I dare not with my own eyes witness this fight between my son and Menelaus, for Zeus and the other immortals alone know which shall fall."[13]

The melancholy and despairing future of man is spoken through Achilles, when King Priam visits him at the end of the

---

12. Homer, *The Iliad* (tr. by Samuel Butler) (New York: Classics Club, 1942), Book III, pp. 47-48.
13. *Iliad*, III:49-50.

11

story begging the body of his slain son Hector for a decent burial. Achilles pities the old man and says,

> Unhappy man . . . Sit now upon this seat, and for all our grief we will hide our sorrows in our hearts, for weeping will not avail us. The immortals know no care, yet the lot they spin for man is full of sorrow. On the floor of Zeus' palace there stand two urns, the one filled with evil gifts, and the other with good ones. He for whom Zeus, the lord of thunder, mixes the gifts he sends, will meet now with good and now with evil fortune; but he to whom Zeus sends none but evil gifts will be pointed at by the finger of scorn, the hand of famine will pursue him to the ends of the world, and he will go up and down the face of the earth, respected neither by gods nor men.[14]

The futility in believing in the Resurrection which Paul pressed in the streets of Athens a few hundred years later is pointed out by Achilles in his vain attempt to comfort old Priam:

> Bear up against it, and let there be some intervals in your sorrow. Mourn as you may for your brave son, you will take nothing by it. You cannot raise him from the dead; ere you do so yet another sorrow shall befall you.[15]

The determinism which really controls the fate of man, whether it be in the hands of the lesser gods, or of the chief god overruling the lesser gods, or in the hands of Fate overruling all the gods, is the principal source of the pessimism which infects a great deal of the *Iliad* and the *Odyssey*. Compared with Homeric determinism, the so-called predestination concepts of St. Augustine, John Calvin, or the American Puritans seem relatively free.

Book XX takes up the tale of the Trojan War at a time when Zeus, the father of the gods, gives his permission for the divinities to take part in the conflict:

---

14. *Iliad,* XXIV:384, 385.
15. *Iliad,* XXIV:385.

So long as the gods held themselves aloof from mortal warriors the Achaeans were triumphant, for Achilles who had long refused to fight was now with them. There was not a Trojan but his limbs failed him for fear as he beheld the fleet son of Peleus all glorious in his armor, and looking like Ares himself. When, however, the Olympians came to take their part among men, forthwith uprose strong Strife, rouser of hosts, and Athene raised her loud voice, now standing by the deep trench that ran outside the wall and now shouting with all her might upon the shore of the sounding sea. Ares also bellowed out upon the other side, dark as some black thundercloud, and called on the Trojans at the top of his voice, now from the acropolis and now speeding up the side of the river Simois, till he came to the hill Callicolone.

Thus did the gods spur on both hosts to fight, and rouse fierce contention also among themselves.[16]

But above even Zeus, father of the gods, stood Fate. In Book XIX Achilles, who had been standing back from the battle because of squabbles within the Greek host, makes ready to return to the war against the Trojans. As he makes his preparation, his gifted horse Xanthus speaks to him:

"Dread Achilles," said he, "we will indeed save you now, but the day of your death is near, and the blame will not be ours, for it will be heaven and stern fate that will destroy you."

. . . . .

When he had thus said the Erinyes stayed his speech, and Achilles answered him in great sadness, saying, "Why, O Xanthus, do you thus foretell my death? You need not do so, for I will know that I am to fall here, far from my dear father and mother; none the more, however, shall I stay my hand till I have given the Trojans their fill of fighting."[17]

---

16. *Iliad*, XX:309-310.
17. *Iliad*, XIX:307.

James Adams in his book, *The Religious Teachers of Greece,* emphasizes that in spite of the belief in Fate and the overruling mechanism of the gods, the Homeric conception of man does not

> degenerate into the inert and hopeless pessimism that bewails with folded hands the miseries of human life. Nothing in his poems can fairly be compared with the pessmistic cry that is often heard in Greek poetry from Theognis onwards: "Best it is not to be born; and next best, being born, to die as soon as possible." On the contrary, it is just the consideration of the weakness and frailty of man, the brevity and uncertainty of human life, which rouses Homer's heroes to their greatest efforts.[18]

HUMANISM AND PLATO

Plato lived c. 429 - 347 B.C. His conception of man is very different from that of Homer. In Platonic thought, the soul and not the body constitutes the essence of man. The older philosophers—Heraclitus, Anaxagoras, the Pythagoreans, and perhaps most of all his teacher, Socrates—contributed to the refinement of the Platonic system which has perhaps been the greatest single influence in the development of Greco-European humanism. Through the city of Alexandria in Egypt, Platonic doctrine is thought to have exerted some influence upon St. Augustine and other Christian thinkers, and the various Romantic movements in literature have tended to revive Plato's ideas either in their original form or in modified form through his third-century A.D. interpreter, Plotinus.

Man, according to Plato, is "a soul using a body."[19] To him, a concept is more real and thus more valuable than the materialistic realization of the concept in matter. The soul of man lives on fully after his physical death, and there are strong suggestions

---

18. James Adam, *The Religious Teachers of Greece* (Edinburgh: T. & T. Clark, 1909), pp. 66-67. Quoted in Babbage, *Op. Cit.,* p. 25.

19. Plato, *Alcibiades,* i, 130c, quoted in Babbage, *Op. Cit.,* p. 26.

that some of his best impulses relate to his memory of pure ideas which he experienced before becoming a physical body. In the spirit of Plato's teacher, Socrates (who himself wrote no surviving books but lives through his student), he teaches the values of the good over the pleasant, the true over the false, and of absolute ideas over sense experience. Wisdom is the pearl of great price which is to be most valued and which remains within a person's soul at death.

In the *Phaedo,* the dialogue where Plato describes the last hours of Socrates before his drinking the hemlock, a stark contrast between the ideal and physical, the soul and body is drawn home; Socrates asks his disciple:

> Yet once more consider the matter in another light. When the soul and the body are united, then nature orders the soul to rule and govern, and the body to obey and serve. Now which of these two functions is akin to the divine? and which to the mortal? Does not the divine appear to you to be that which naturally orders and rules, and the mortal to be that which is subject and servant?
>
> True.
>
> And which does the soul resemble?
>
> The soul resembles the divine, and the body the mortal— there can be no doubt of that, Socrates.
>
> Then reflect, Cebes, of all which has been said is not this the conclusion?—that the soul is in the very likeness of the divine, and immortal, and intellectual, and uniform, and indissoluble, and unchangeable; and that the body is in the very likeness of the human, and mortal, and unintellectual, and multiform, and dissoluble, and changeable. Can this, my dear Cebes, be denied?
>
> It cannot.
>
> But if it be true, then is not the body liable to speedy dissolution? and is not the soul almost or altogether indissoluble?
>
> Certainly.

And do you further observe, that after a man is dead, the body, or visible part of him, which is lying in the visible world, and is called a corpse, and would naturally be dissolved and decomposed and dissipated, is not dissolved or decomposed at once, but may remain for some time, nay even for a long time, if the constitution be sound at the time of death, and the season of the year favorable? For the body, when shrunk and embalmed, as the manner is in Egypt, may remain almost entire through infinite ages; and even in decay, there are still some portions, such as the bones and ligaments, which are practically indestructible. Do you agree?

Yes.

And is it likely that the soul, which is invisible, in passing to the place of the true Hades, which like her is invisible, and pure, and noble, and on her way to the good and wise God, whither, if God will, my soul is also soon to go—that the soul, I repeat, if this be her nature and origin, will be blown away and destroyed immediately on quitting the body, as the many say? That can never be, my dear Simmias and Cebes. The truth rather is, that the soul which is pure at departing and draws after her no bodily taint, have never voluntarily during life had connection with the body, which she is ever avoiding, herself gathered into herself; and making such abstraction her perpetual study—which means that she has been a true disciple of philosophy; and therefore has in fact been always engaged in the practice of dying—for is not philosophy the study of death?[20]

Socrates proceeds to contrast the blissful future of the soul which is pure, and the endless wandering of the polluted soul in search of a home because it is unable to let go of its bodily ideas and principles. There is a strong hint of reincarnation at this point in the Socratic-Platonic theology or philosophy.

It is impossible to avoid making some comparisons between Platonic dualism—the polarity he sees between body and spirit —and that dualism expressed by St. Paul, for example, in the

20. Plato, *Phaedo* (New York: Walter J. Black, 1942), pp. 114-115.

Letter to the Romans as he expresses his desperation to be released from the "body of this death."[21] The difference is wide, however, when one recognizes the *Imago Dei* concept in Pauline theology—the realization that Christ redeems the total person and not just the soul. Paul speaks of the groans of creation awaiting the redemption of our bodies, and the great fifteenth chapter of First Corinthians speaks of *this mortal* putting on immortality. Ultimately, Platonic humanism is much more pessimistic than the Christian acceptance of the Fall through Adam's sin, coupled with the redemption of all creation through the Second Adam, Jesus Christ.

HUMANISM IN ARISTOTLE

Aristotle, who was for a time a student of Plato, shared with his teacher a certain contempt for the ordinary man and a respect for wisdom and knowledge which glorified the aristocratic person.[22] As a biologist, he seems to have had more appreciation for the physical and living organism than Plato, however. Man attains his highest fulfillment in society rather than as an individual, and thus he is very interested in the ethical possibilities of politics. In the *Nichomachean Ethics* Aristotle discusses the "function of Man" and decides that it should be an activity of soul in accordance with reason.[23] He refers to three types of life, the sensual, the political, and the rational, or life of thought.[24] Of these three, the rational is easily the highest and most valuable and is to be cultivated by the person seeking the meaning of life. Aristotle also prefers values which are intrinsically good to those which are merely instrumental in securing secondary objects or values. Happiness, for example, fulfills this criterion and is therefore much to be desired.[25]

---

21. Romans 7:24.
22. Babbage, p. 31.
23. Aristotle, *Nichomachean Ethics,* tr. by James E. C. Welldon (New York: Walter J. Black for The Classics Club, 1943), p. 88.
24. *Ibid.,* p. 89.
25. *Ibid.,* p. 91.

Aristotle is very specific in supporting the ancient Greek ideal of the golden mean—the lack of fanaticism in any direction—as a definition of the good:

> Virtue then is a state of deliberate moral purpose, consisting in a mean relative to ourselves, the mean being determined by reason, or as a prudent man would determine it. It is a mean, firstly, as lying between two vices, the vice of excess on the one hand, and the vice of deficiency on the other, and, secondly, because whereas the vices either fall short of or go beyond what is right in emotion and action, virtue discovers and chooses the mean.[26]

Happiness, according to Aristotle, is not mere amusement, but is the joy which is found in rationality. Babbage criticizes this aspect of classic humanism with a quotation from the Christian existentialist, Søren Kierkegaard:

> It is this excessive intellectualism which leads the Greeks to equate sin with ignorance. Sin is simply a form of mental blindness: He who knows what is right, does it. It is as simple as all that. It is against this Socratic conception of sin that Søren Kierkegaard, in the name of Christianity, utters his impassioned protest.
>
> "Socrates explains that he who does not do the right thing has not understood it; but Christianity goes a little further back and says, it is not because he will not understand it, and in turn is because he does not will the right. And in the next place, describing what properly is defiance, it teaches that a man does wrong although he understands what is right, or forbears to do right although he understands what is right.
>
> "So then, Christianity understood, sin lies in the will, not in the intellect; and this corruption of the will goes well beyond the consciousness of the individual."[27]

---

26. *Ibid.,* p. 109.
27. Kierkegaard, *The Sickness unto Death,* tr. by Walter Lowrie, Princeton University Press, 1941, pp. 154-155. Quoted in Babbage, *Op. Cit.,* p. 32.

One other important aspect of Aristotle's thought is important for American Christians who live within the context of the Campbell-Stone Restoration Movement. Aristotle's logic, together with his dualistic understanding of body and mind, was utilized heavily by St. Thomas Aquinas in his formulation of Christian doctrine called *Scholasticism* during the eleventh century. This heavy emphasis upon the rational process, though modified by the Reformation and by the Enlightenment, John Locke and Thomas Jefferson, emerged as a vigorous factor in the first hundred years of the Restoration Movement in America. The debates of Alexander Campbell helped to establish the Disciples of Christ as a respectable movement in the midsection of America, and the heritage of debate and the rational process were still alive and well in certain fragments of the Churches of Christ by the middle of this century.

STOIC AND EPICUREAN HUMANISM

A word is still needed about the Stoic and Epicurean streams of philosophy which were present in Athens at Paul's visit at about 49 or 50 A.D. Both philosophies are primarily concerned with ethical motivation rather than with metaphysics, or the great questions about the nature of being in itself. Babbage summarizes the Epicurean outlook in these words:

> The pleasure which Epicurus commends is peaceful serenity rather than excessive enjoyment. The happy man is the man who is free from pain of body and trouble of mind. The test of true pleasure is the absence of all that gives pain or causes fear. The natural instinct which prompts a man to seize an immediate enjoyment is held in check by a prudential consideration of the consequences. Feeling is subordinated to reason, which adjudicates between competing pleasures with a view to achieving tranquility of mind.[28]

---

28. Babbage, p. 34.

Though there is a strong base of philosophical hedonism contained in this description, reason still is lord over the physical and emotional feelings, and the old concept of *sophrosyne,* the avoidance of excess and the seeking of moderation, remains central. Compared with Paul's Gospel, there is a strong sense of passivity in comparison with the activism for human redemption present in the Christian message.

Stoicism, on the other hand, teaches that the chief good of mankind is not pleasure but goodness. As with Aristotle, the life of virtue is the life of reason.

Stoicism was founded at the close of the fourth century B.C. by Zeno and is called Stoicism because of the painted corridor on the north side of the market place at Athens, called the Stoa, where Zeno gave his lectures. This site was probably one which the Apostle Paul viewed on his entrance to the city before going to the Areopagus. Stoicism accepted the dualism of Socrates— the soul is far superior to the body, and is ordered by God or by the gods. The strongest historical emphasis is upon ethics— moral behavior reflecting the life of reason, and the willingness to subjugate the body to the vicissitudes of life because the soul is the essence of humanity.

The first-century group of Stoics was perhaps most clearly characterized by Seneca, a contemporary of Paul, whose exchange of letters with the apostle is a part of tradition if not of history. Seneca describes the body as "a mere husk or fetter or prison of the soul; with its departure begins the soul's true life."[29]

Epictetus and the Roman emperor Marcus Aurelius were also latter-day disciples of Stoicism. Epictetus called man "a son of God"[30] and Marcus Aurelius emphasized the existence of "a kinship, a community of mind."[31]

---

29. Robert D. Hicks, "Stoics" in *Encyclopaedia Britannica* (Chicago: Encyclopaedia Britannica, Inc., 1963). V. 21.

30. Babbage, p. 35.

31. *Ibid.*

Babbage summarizes Seneca's stoicism in this discouraging statement:

Seneca understands man's moral weakness, but he has no cure for man's sickness. His only prescription is a cold and stern moralism. The passions and appetites cannot be directed; they can only be crushed.

Nevertheless, it is impossible to withhold admiration from the Stoic conception of the ideal man. Seneca's noble and moving *confessio fidei* is typical of Stoicism at its best:

"I will look upon death or upon comedy, with the same expression of countenance. I will submit to labors however great they may be, supporting the strength of my body by that of my mind. I will despise riches when I have them as much as when I have them not. Whether fortune comes or goes, I will take no notice of her. I will view all lands as though they belong to me, and my own as though they belonged to all mankind. I will so live as to remember that I was born for others, and will thank nature on this account; for in what fashion could she have done better for me? She has given me alone to all, and all to me alone. Whatever I may possess, I will think that I have no possessions so real as those which I have given away to deserving people. I never will consider a gift to be a large one if it be bestowed upon a worthy object. I will do nothing because of public opinion, but everything because of conscience.[32]

I do not find classical humanism a radical enemy of the Gospel nor do I find it unproductive for the study of Christians. The Church has always interacted with it, and Western culture is probably a strong blend of Judaeo-Christian teaching with classic humanism. In many ways it might almost be said that Socrates and his students provided a world view which facilitated the highway for the Gospel of the Son of God.

Classic humanism generally supported the supremacy of the ideal good, the importance of the spirit over the body, and the

32. Seneca, *Dialogues,* vii, 20, quoted in Babbage, pp. 36-37.

higher value of things spiritual over the material world. The extremely high value set upon the intellect and the rational process, however, tend to set up an aristocracy of the wise which the lowly Son of Man did not embrace and His disciples cannot accept.

Paul went from Athens, perhaps in some discouragement, to another Greek city, Corinth. Could it have been that he reacted from the intellectualism of Athens' classic humanism when he later wrote,

> When I came to you, brethren, I did not come proclaiming to you the testimony of God in lofty words of wisdom. For I decided to know nothing among you except Jesus Christ and him crucified. And I was with you in weakness and in much fear and trembling; and my speech and my message were not in plausible words of wisdom, but in demonstration of the Spirit and power, that your faith might not rest in the wisdom of men but in the power of God.[33]

Today's Christian, appreciating the high road of classical humanism, still reacts to the confusion of intellectual idolatry with revulsion, particularly when he perceives the spiritual ignorance emanating from the wealth of intellectual strength. The altar inscribed "To an unknown God" still provokes the spirit of one who believes that Jesus is the Way, the Truth, and the Life.

Remembering that Christ loved us when we were yet sinners, that He calls the poor and the lowly as well as the wise and the strong, and that He gives hope for both our spirits and for our immortal bodies throughout Eternity, we might well share the great apostle's sense of disappointment that the intellectuals of Athens were so preoccupied with the wisdom of classic humanism that they scoffed at the Resurrection of Christ, and the only fruits of his labors were "some men" who joined him and believed, "among them Dionysius the Areopagite and a woman named Damaris and others with them."[34]

---

33. I Corinthians 2:1-5 (RSV).
34. Acts 17:34 (RSV).

2

THE IMAGE OF MAN IN RENAISSANCE HUMANISM

In 1835 that young American super-editor, statesman, preacher, debater, farmer, educator, and founding spirit of the American Restoration Movement, Alexander Campbell, published a series of articles in book form which outlined his thinking about Christianity and the Church. Together with his father Thomas Campbell, he had already eschewed a creedal basis for the Church and had condemned that approach as divisive and a barrier to the unity of Christians sought by his movement. As his later debates with the New Harmony socialist Robert Owen, the Catholic Bishop Purcell, and his numerous other opponents clearly demonstrate, Campbell was in no way opposed to the logical process. The very title of the new book, *The Christian System,* underlies the methodical thought which characterized his approach to applying evidence to belief.[1] In contemporary

1. Alexander Campbell, *The Christian System* (Cincinnati: Standard Publishing Co., n.d.)

learning terms, Campbell might be considered to have leaned more to the cognitive and the intellectual domain than to the affective and to human emotion.

The collection of articles in *The Christian System* clearly demonstrates Campbell's acceptance of universal truths, an acceptance he shared not only with the New Testament writers and the classical Greek humanists, but also with the medieval Church. In the "Preface" to the book he speaks of his own personal battle between his opinions and the logically-derived general principles he espouses:

> We were not, indeed, at first apprized of the havoc which our *principles* would make upon our *opinions*. We soon, however, found our principles and opinions at war on some points; and the question immediately arose, *Whether shall we sacrifice our principles to our opinions, or our opinions to our principles?* We need not say that we were compelled to the latter, judging that our principles were better than our opinions. Hence, since we put to sea on board this bottom, we have been compelled to throw overboard some opinions once as dear to us as they now are to those who never thought of the difference between principle and opinion.[2]

The practice of the Restoration Movement in "fighting error" through debate and intellectual controversy, attempting to demolish subjective personal opinions through the logical application of principles of binding argument, became one of the keystones of the Disciple Movement before the middle of the nineteenth century. In my own youth, the pride which leading Church of Christ preachers took in "demolishing the Baptists" or other people considered to be muddling in error manifested a continuation of the old faith in cognitive logic. From a psychological viewpoint, to say nothing of the primary New Testament preference for love (a feeling) over intellectual mastery, this one-sided emphasis upon doctrinal perfection with relative disregard

---

2. Alexander Campbell, xv.

for peoples' feelings manifested through their opinions may have torpedoed the basic Restoration objective of unifying the Church of Christ before the Movement got fully off the ground. But the emphasis is a direct descendant of medieval Scholasticism and serves to provide a backdrop for our study of Renaissance Humanism.

MEDIEVAL SCHOLASTICISM

Medieval Scholasticism represented the Church's fusion of Biblical principle with classical logic—particularly the logic of Aristotle. Particularly binding from late in the eleventh century through most of the fourteenth, Scholasticism received its most sophisticated formulation by St. Thomas Aquinas who lived during the thirteenth century. Babbage notes that it was the good Scholastic Doctor who "set himself to the prodigious task of reconciliation; he sought to harmonize, as far as possible, the exciting speculations of Aristotle with the truths of Biblical revelation."[3]

It will be remembered that for Aristotle, the body and the soul are quite separate from each other, even opposed to each other. Immortality belongs only to the mind. Aquinas, however, holds that the soul, though it is immortal, cannot "exercise all its potentialities in separation from the body."[4] In speaking of this principle, he says:

> It is contrary to the nature of the soul to be without the body. But nothing which is contrary to nature can be perpetual. Hence the soul will not forever be without the body. Therefore since the soul remains forever, it should be united again with the body, and this is what is meant by rising (from the dead). The immortality of souls seems to demand the future resurrection of bodies.[5]

---

3. Stuart Barton Babbage, *Man in Nature and in Grace* (Grand Rapids: Wm. B. Eerdmans Publishing Co., 1957), p. 46.
4. *Ibid.*, p. 47.
5. Aquinas, *Summa contra Gentiles*, 4, 79.

In speaking of the freedom-predestination problem later addressed by the sixteenth-century reformers, Aquinas retained the logical emphasis of Aristotle. Babbage summarizes several of his statements in the following passage:

> He lays strong emphasis on reason's function in free choice. Free choice, he says, is an act of the will resulting from a judgment of reason. If man were not free, "counsels, exhortations, precepts, prohibitions, rewards and punishments would be pointless." In accordance with this belief in man's innate rationality is the doctrine that all created things tend towards the actualization of their potentialities; in the case of human beings not only instinctively, but also by means of intellect and will.[6]

From a Biblical point of view, it might be suggested that the school men attempted literally to put the new wine of Christian faith into the old bottles of classical philosophy and logic. The unsigned article on "Scholasticism" in the 1963 edition of the *Encyclopaedia Britannica* suggests that "We might say with . . . truth that the philosophy of St. Thomas is Aristotle Christianized. The Schoolmen contemplate the universe of nature and man not with their own eyes but in the glass of Aristotelian formulae."[7] And summarizing the problems of the Scholastics, the same author suggests, "But this is equivalent to a confession that Scholasticism had failed in its task, which was to rationalize the doctrines of the church. The Aristotelian form of Christian theology refused to be forced into an alien form."[8]

C. S. Lewis, who acknowledges his own debt to Thomas Aquinas, is highly critical of any theology which attempts too tightly to describe and contain God. In *Mere Christianity* Lewis says, "In the long run God is no one but Himself and what He

---

6. Babbage, p. 48.

7. *Encyclopaedia Britannica* (Chicago: Encyclopaedia Britannica, Inc., 1963), xx, 81.

8. *Ibid.,* xx, 82.

does is like nothing else." And in his *Letters to Malcolm,* he says, "Every idea of Him we form, He must in mercy shatter." And he mentions that Thomas Aquinas once said of his own theology, "It reminds me of straw."[9]

THE RENAISSANCE

With this backdrop of medieval theology, we turn to the elusive problem of trying to define the Renaissance in time and in qualities. Since a given definition and a specific geography determine the period of Euro-history under consideration, for our purposes we will arbitrarily mark out the period from approximately the middle of the fifteenth century to the end of the sixteenth.

Mayer, in his *History of Philosophy,* suggests that the Renaissance can be regarded from two viewpoints:

> First, it was a backward look to Greece and Rome; many of the humanists, especially Erasmus, regarded Greek culture as the supreme achievement in Western civilization. Yet, there was another feature of the Renaissance which was truly progressive and forward-looking. By stressing the importance of this world, by emphasizing the dignity of man, by championing the possibilities of reason, Renaissance scholars pointed to a new scientific age and laid the foundations for our own period.[10]

Matthew Spinka suggests that "Modern history, particularly the history of ideas, has its true beginning in the Renaissance. This was not merely a period of 'awakening the dead' of antiquity, of a mere resuscitation of the antique culture, but of the birth of modern man."[11] He goes on to comment that "Much that is

---

9. William Luther White, *The Image of Man in C. S. Lewis* (Nashville and New York: Abingdon Press, 1969), pp. 38-39.

10. Frederick Mayer, *A History of Modern Philosophy* (New York: American Book Company, 1951), p. 11.

11. Matthew Spinka, *Christian Thought from Erasmus to Berdyaev* (Englewood Cliffs, N.J.: Prentice-Hall, Inc., 1962), p. 5.

noble and of permanent value has been produced during those six centuries. Human liberties, rights of man, liberal constitutions guaranteeing inalienable rights and freedoms, have been secured during this time."[12] Further defining the period outlined above, Spinka continues:

> The new orientation has been humanistic, or as Jacques Maritain speaks of it, 'anthropocentric.' "The proper study of mankind is man" is the motto of the Renaissance. Man became the measure of all things—man and his place in nature. The two went hand in hand. If medieval man lived an anonymous life, not yet clearly differentiated from the group of which he was part, Renaissance man attained individuality (although not always personality). Medieval man lived much more consciously in relation to God, or rather the Church, which mediated the supernatural life to him through the sacramental system. . . . It was then in the early Renaissance that the spirit of humanism was born, the spirit of self-assertion, of this-worldliness, of scientific study of nature, and of human autonomy. . . . Hence, the chief interest of the age was humanistic.[13]

The *Renaissance* and *humanism* are both many-sided terms which illustrate the need for us to study several facets of the subject if we wish to intelligently counter some of the anti-Christian advances of certain types of humanism. Bernard O'Kelly, in his Introduction to a collection of essays on the Renaissance, suggests that we like to pretend that most of our own past (or specifically the Renaissance) had a kind of simplicity and completeness which it did not actually possess. The danger, he says, "lies in settling with too much finality upon one or two (or five or eleven) significant keys to the understanding of the Renaissance and then trying to make all the doors fit the keys."[14] Further,

---

12. *Ibid.*, pp. 5-6.
13. *Ibid.*, p. 6.
14. Bernard O'Kelly, "Introduction" from *The Renaissance Image of Man and the World* (Columbus: Ohio State University Press, 1966), p. 9.

he says, "There is no truth about the Renaissance—there are truths, an almost infinite number of them, and some of them ought to seem to us very strange bedfellows indeed."[15]

RENAISSANCE HUMANISM

Renaissance humanism is also very difficult to organize into neat rows of thought. Evolving from the early Italian Renaissance when one of the principal characteristics might have been its interest in classical studies, until the late Italian Renaissance and the North German awakening to the humanities, when one of the dominant interests seems to have been interest in modernity, humanism is also a many-splendored concept.

Of primary interest to us here is its interest in and relationship to Christianity. Douglas Bush underlines the basic Christian vein of thought which permeates a great deal of Renaissance humanism: "Much Renaissance thought and literature cannot be understood if we slight the continuing impulse to reconcile nature and grace, pagan reason and Christian faith."[16] Again, he acknowledges, "Modern writers have often spoken of *studia humanitatis* as if the name implied opposition to theology; sometimes it did, but in the orthodox view these studies were complementary, not antagonistic. As Cicero, the oracle and model of Renaissance humanism, had said, *sapietia* is the knowledge of things human and divine. Or, as Aquinas had said, grace does not abolish nature but perfects it."[17]

Warnock and Anderson, among others who have written about Renaissance humanism, seem to me to overstate the contrast between the Middle Ages and the Renaissance. Speaking of the late Middle Ages, they say:

---

15. *Ibid.*
16. Douglas Bush, "The Renaissance: The Literary Climate" in O'Kelly, ed., *The Renaissance Image of Man and the World* (Columbus: Ohio State University Press, 1966), p. 70.
17. *Ibid.*, p. 71.

The Greek language and hence its literature were practically forgotten in the West, and not only the classical drama but the very concept of acting and the stage were lost. Even the few ancients who struggled through were largely misunderstood, because the religious mind of the Middle Ages, bound up in mystical symbols and lacking historical perspective, interposed a barrier of Christian theology between itself and the ancient past. Achilles and Aeneas became chivalrous knights with armor and lance, and the Hades of Virgil was transformed into a Christian hell. Hence the "renaissance" of the ancients was not simply a rediscovery of the ancient classics from oblivion. It was the rebirth of an understanding of the ancients in their own terms, freed from the veil of medieval mysticism. Only the revival of secular culture made possible this new perspective divorced from theology and symbolism.[18]

It seems clear that one characteristic of the Italian humanism which emerged during the early Renaissance was its continued tendency to interpret classical Greek and Roman themes in terms of Christian Theology.

There is a parallelism here between the competing theology of the Catholic Church, sometimes called Scholasticism or Thomism, and the humanistic thrust of the Renaissance. Thomism attempted to blend Aristotle with the teachings of the Bible and the religion of Christ. Humanism interpreted ancient classical themes as Christian symbols. Although Thomism and humanism were competitive ideas in their own time, they were parallel in their mutual attempt to blend what seems to us the incompatible. Richard Hooker, the Anglican who was instrumental in framing much of the theology of the English reformation, pointed out the dual revelation of God in the Word and in Nature: "The general and perpetual voice of men is as the

---

18. Robert Warnock and George K. Anderson, "Humanism and the New Learning," *The World in Literature* (Chicago: Scott, Foresman and Company, 1950 (1959), pp. 528-529.

sentence of God himself. For that which all men have at all times learned, Nature herself must needs have taught; and God being the author of Nature, her voice is but his instrument."[19] Bush suggests that Hooker's words here explain the philosophic "basis of Christian humanism, the rational Christian's acceptance of pagan thought as, with all its deficiencies, a partial anticipation and natural ally of Christian faith."[20]

One characteristic of Renaissance humanism, at least early in the Italian Renaissance, seems to have been a desire on the part of people to leap over the ages out of which they derived their immediate history and to return to the pure font of learning, the classical period before Christ. The great Renaissance scholar, Paul Kristeller, suggests,

> As you well know, the humanists looked with respect and admiration upon classical antiquity and more or less bitterly attacked the Middle Ages; they tried in many ways to imitate the former and to abandon the traditions of the latter. In countless statements . . . the humanists spoke of the ancient eloquence and poetry, letters and arts, learning and wisdom that were being reborn in their own time after a long period of decay and that were being brought back to light after the darkness of many centuries.[21]

This humanistic push to refuse to acknowledge a people's immediate history and to attempt to make the leap back to a purer source and an earlier period is certainly not unique to the Renaissance. Students of the Restoration Movement in America are acquainted with the parallel concept developed by the Disciples after the original Campbell-Stone generation—a concept which spoke of *Restoration* rather than *Reformation*. For

---

19. Quoted in Bush, *op. cit.,* p. 72.
20. *Ibid.*
21. Paul O. Kristeller, "Philosophy and Humanism in Renaissance Perspective," in O'Kelly, ed., *The Renaissance Image of Man and the World* (Columbus: Ohio State University Press, 1966), p. 36.

example, M. M. Davis in his little book, *How the Disciples Begin and Grew,* suggests of the nineteenth-century American religious movement,

> The principle involved was one of the loftiest that ever animated men: it was an unselfish attempt to restore primitive Christianity. At great cost, and with no material reward in view, these brave men, despite the greatest difficulties, began the search for the old paths.[22]

Walter Scott often spoke of "the Gospel restored" but Alexaander and Thomas Campbell usually used the term, "the ancient order of things" to describe their ideal, the Biblically-described church of Christ. Alexander Campbell himself often spoke more modestly of reformation rather than restoration, however, and in many ways acknowledged the reforming grace of Martin Luther. In the preface to *The Christian System,* he says:

> We Americans owe our national privileges and our civil liberties to the Protestant reformers. They achieved not only an imperishable fame for themselves, but a rich legacy for their posterity. When we contrast the present state of these United States with Spanish America, and the condition of the English nation with that of Spain, Portugal, and Italy, we begin to appreciate how much we are indebted to the intelligence, faith, and courage of Martin Luther and his heroic associates in that glorious reformation.[23]

But Campbell's acknowledgement of history and the sources of his own religious and political heritage was not shared by all the later generations of Restorationist preachers and members. Like some of the more extreme humanists of the Renaissance, many people involved in the movement he began did not realize that while they were reaching for Biblical purity

---

22. M. M. Davis, *How the Disciples Began and Grew* (Cincinnati: The Standard Publishing Company, 1915), p. 229.
23. Campbell, *Op. Cit.,* p. vii.

and pure Christian origins, they were also products of all the history which had interposed itself between the apostles and Alexander Campbell.

Renaissance humanism borrows from the classical Greeks the concept of the dignity, supremacy, and intellectual power of Mankind. As Babbage suggests, the body was the "joy of life" to Homer and "Nothing is so desirable as a robust physical frame."[24] Renaissance humanistic sculpture and literature reach back into classic antiquity for this image of robust man. In keeping with their dual understanding, Renaissance humanists derived their proud image of Man from *both* the Greek model and from their Judeo-Christian belief that Man was created *imago Dei,* in the image of God. Thus the reconciliation of pagan and Christian sources continued.

Theologically, it can be seen that Mankind was viewed less and less in the way Saint Augustine had described him a thousand years earlier when he suggested that Man can only will that which is evil, and the fall of Adam had infected all men with a fatal taint.[25] In the spirit of Paul's letter to the Romans, Chapter VII, Augustine concluded that no human power can deliver a person from his hereditary depravity and the gift of life is the work of the grace of God.[26] Salvation is only of God. All have sinned and come short of the glory of God.[27]

In my opinion, this is the most important aspect of Renaissance humanism, this change in understanding of Man's innate condition from helpless and fallen sinner to proud, upright and robust man who wears his innate badge of physical and intellectual beauty because he is created in God's very image. This philosophical outlook served to help trigger the Protestant Reformation during the fifteenth and sixteenth centuries.

---

24. Babbage, p. 24.
25. *Ibid.,* p. 41.
26. *Ibid.*
27. *Ibid.*

Summarizing some of the characteristics of humanism of the fifteenth and sixteenth centuries, these traits seem important for our understanding of the concept:

1. A glorified view of the Greek and Roman classic authors and artists and an attempt to recreate the spirit of literature and art from classic humanism.

2. An attempt to integrate the pagan forms of classic literature, art, and philosophy into Christian forms and Biblical understanding, often as "teaching aids" for the support of organized Christianity.

3. A belief in the innate dignity and perfectability of Mankind.

4. A tendency toward civic involvement and lives of action although there is still some lip service to the life of contemplation.

The literature of the Renaissance, as well as the art, architecture and music produced by the humanists, reflects forms, themes, and philosophical positions which are in sharp contrast to earlier periods of European writing. Dante and Petrarch were able to relate the theme of human romantic love to religious and spiritual allegories; Boccaccio not only pursued the study of the Greek classics but produced an almost ribald collection of anecdotes in his *Decameron*. Pico della Mirandola reflected the new humanism in his spirited defense of the dignity of man. Lorenzo de'Medici not only supported literature and the arts in his native Florence but in his own poetry produced what J. A. Symonds has called some of the "first absolutely modern work."[28] The great Dutch humanist, Erasmus, English Catholic humanist Sir Thomas More, the Spanish satirical writer Miguel de Cervantes, Italian philosopher Niccolo Machiavelli, and the English masters Geoffrey Chaucer, John Milton, John Donne, Edmund Spenser, and Christopher Marlowe, share with William Shakespeare credit for what has to be considered a golden age of literature.

---

28. J. A. Symonds, "Renaissance" in *Encyclopaedia Britannica* (Chicago: Encyclopaedia Britannica, 1963), XIX:126.

The allegory, which utilizes the basic duality of metaphorical language, was represented consummately in Edmund Spenser's *The Faerie Queen*. The combination of Christian virtue with humanistic and pagan characters interacting through allegorical names and situations provides an ultimate example of English Renaissance humanism, a humanism which still retains the flavor of Christianity but mingles it with forms and concepts derived from a more earthy world.

The debate about Shakespeare has raged long and warm. With his worldly ability to portray people in their this-world environment and his humanistic grasp of worldly philosophy, was he basically motivated by Christian faith? This enigmatic question is a microcosm of the larger problems in an attempt to define or label Renaissance humanism.

A question of primary interest to us is the matter of the possible relationship between Renaissance humanism and the Protestant Reformation. Here, as in other matters of the philosophy of humanism, one encounters a wide difference of opinion, but my own is that humanism both helped trigger the Reformation and was antithetical to it. First, humanism had supported the development of a large public who could read for themselves. Second, the study of original manuscripts which motivated the entire humanist movement, the emphasis upon origins and the hunger to learn from the original documents, seems to have been transferred from the classical scholars studying Greek manuscripts to churchmen who became interested in studying the Bible and learning more of first-century Christianity. A. G. Dickens writes, "Even the briefest account of the intellectual forces which underlay the Reformation could not ignore the decline of philosophical theology and its replacement by a new type of biblical theology based upon humanist scholarship. . . ."[29] J. A. Symonds some years ago contended:

29. A. G. Dickens, *Reformation and Society in Sixteenth-Century Europe* (London: Thames and Hudson with Harcourt, Brace and Co., Inc., 1966), p. 29.

The point of contact between humanism and the Reformation has to be insisted on; for it is just here that the relation of the Reformation to the Renaissance in general makes itself apparent. . . . The touch of the new spirit which had evolved literature, art and culture in Italy sufficed in Germany to recreate Christianity. This new spirit in Italy emancipated human intelligence by the classics; in Germany it emancipated the human conscience by the Bible. . . . The Reformation, inspired by the same energy of resuscitated life as the Renaissance, assisted by the same engines of the printing-press and paper, using the same apparatus of scholarship, criticism, literally skill, being in truth another manifestation of the same world movement under a diverse form, now posed itself as an irreconcilable antagonist to Renaissance Italy. . . . The truth is that the Reformation was the Teutonic Renaissance.[30]

And Andre Chastel agrees:

Within the framework of the Church, humanism set itself up as an organ of criticism; it took up the ideas of the Catholic reformation and repeated, with variations and in another key, those of 15th century heresies. This was evident in the case of Erasmus. All such tendencies did help, in a way, to prepare the ground for the immediate success of Luther and the Reformers. Having revived the old heretical doctrines, they found in humanism the instrument and universal language lacking to Wycliff and to Huss. . . . 'Erasmus laid the egg and Luther hatched it,' they were to say later; a characteristic error in perspective.[31]

Although there are scholars who take issue with this point of view, it seems clear that the tools of thought, research, and writing transmitted by the humanists to the reformers helped make possible the alternate view of Christianity, the emphasis upon the Scriptures, and the polemic and writing skills which

---

30. Symonds, XIX:129.
31. Andre Chastel, *The Age of Humanism* (New York: McGraw-Hill Book Company, Inc., 1963), p. 16.

were basic to the Protestant Reformation. As we critique the concept of humanism, therefore, we need to note that in the fifteenth and sixteenth centuries it was in some ways a creative force which must have been used "in the fulness of time" to emancipate Christians from the doctrines, practices, and mental stranglehold which the Roman Church maintained at the end of the Middle Ages.

Another thrust of Renaissance humanism seems to have been the emphasis upon wholeness in mental outlook, a unified world view, which study of the humanities was supposed to help undergird and support. Kristeller points out that the period did not use the term "humanism" but did coin the terms "humanist" and "humanities."[32]

> If we take the Renaissance description of the humanities seriously, as I am inclined to do, we shall understand why the work of the humanists spans the territory of several disciplines that have been distinct in modern times: humanists were classical scholars and historians, poets and prose writers, literary critics and political theorists, and they were philosophers, especially moral philosophers. The contribution each humanist made to any of these fields varies greatly in quality and quantity; yet it is important to realize that for a Renaissance humanist they form a connected, if not unified, whole which he was inclined to consider as his proper domain.[33]

The fragmentation of thought in the "smorgasbord" approach to studies offered by the typical modern university often lacks the unifying strength offered by the Renaissance humanities in helping a student organize his beliefs, his understandings, and his life. In this sense, at least, I would not be in the least offended to be called a "Christian humanist."

But there remains one sharp distinction between Biblical Christianity and Renaissance humanism which marks a basic

---

32. Kristeller, p. 31.
33. *Ibid.*, p. 31.

watershed between them. The difference hinges on Paul's summary of three of the Psalms in the third chapter of his letter to the Romans:

> None is righteous, no not one;
>   no one understands, no one seeks for God,
> All have turned aside, together they have gone wrong;
>   no one does good, not even one.
> Their throat is an open grave,
>   they use their tongues to deceive.
> The venom of asps is under their lips.
> Their mouth is full of curses and bitterness.
> Their feet are swift to shed blood,
>   in their paths are ruin and misery
>   and the way of peace they do not know.
> There is no fear of God before their eyes.[34]

Contrary to the humanist vision of *Homo sapiens* walking proudly on two legs with his athletic frame, his intellectual powers and his strong moral purpose, Paul through the Spirit summarizes the human condition in the simple words, "Since all have sinned and fall short of the glory of God, they are justified by his grace as a gift, through the redemption which is in Christ Jesus, whom God put forward as an expiation by his blood, to be received by faith."[35]

It is understandable that Martin Luther and the reformers regarded the letter to the Romans, together with that to the Galatians, as central in their rejection of both Thomistic Scholasticism with its great fusion of Aristotle and Churchly tradition on the one hand, and of proud humanism on the other. Jacques Maritain, the great Catholic humanist of the twentieth century, correctly understands the contrast between the Protestant doctrine of the grace of God extended toward fallen Man, and

---

34. Romans 3:10-18 (RSV).
35. Romans 3:23-25a (RSV).

integral man lifting himself toward God by his intelligence and devotion, even though Maritain is, from my perspective, on the wrong side of the argument:

> If St. Augustine is interpreted in a material sense, with the simple lights of a reason not truly theological but geometrical, it seems that in his doctrine the creature is annihilated. Man, by original sin, is *essentially corrupted*—it is the doctrine of Luther, of Calvin, of Jansenius.[36]

Forgetting, it seems to me, Paul's cry of celebration, "I have been crucified with Christ, it is no longer I who live, but Christ who lives in me,"[37] Maritain goes on to say:

> Such is the dialectic and the tragedy of the Protestant conscience, with its admirably ardent and sorrowful—yet itself purely human, tenebrously human—sense of human misery and of sin. The creature declares its nothingness!
>
> . . . . .
>
> The problem of grace and freedom receives likewise a simple and even simplistic solution: there is no longer any free will; it has been killed by original sin. It is, in short, the doctrine of predestination and reprobation in the sense of the Protestant schools, the theology of *grace without freedom*.[38]

Dickens describes the growing tension between Luther and Erasmus, who early in Luther's career had been supportive, as the contrast between Erasmus' belief in the dignity and goodness of man clashed with the Lutheran doctrine of salvation by grace.

Whether or not such concepts were anti-Catholic, they were certainly anti-Aristotelian and anti-humanist. Presently they

---

36. Jacques Maritain, *Integral Humanism* (South Bend, Indiana: University of Notre Dame Press, 1968 (1973), p. 16.

37. *Ibid.*

38. *Ibid.*, p. 17.

brought Luther into conflict with Erasmus, who as a good humanist believed in the basic dignity and goodness of man, in man's ability by the exercise of free will to contribute towards his own salvation. In 1525 Luther accordingly directed his *Bondage of the Will* against Erasmus in particular and humanist Christianity in general.[39]

That the ideal fusion between classic humanism and the Biblical *Imago Dei* rarely occurred in fact is suggested by G. G. Coulton in his references to artistic motivations. Quoting Perrens' *History of Florence,* he says:

> That Brunelleschi had lost what a few may call the sentiment of religion, which is only the tradition of heiratic art of ancient times, we need not doubt.* He built churches and palaces upon the same antique models. . . . But, like Giotto, he had the taste for natural forms. . . . He advanced art in the direction of truth and reality, and, in building temples for churches, incurred, like many others, the reproach of being a pagan. Not an unjustifiable reproach, certainly, but those who flung it at the fifteenth century ought to have included the fourteenth also. . . .
>
> If Giotto, of joyous and pagan temperament, only painted sacred and serious subjects, it was because he did not solely paint for pleasure, but also for bread" . . . Benozzo Gozzoli was a skeptic, ready to work either in the religious or the profane style; Perugino's religious skepticism was notorious and impenitent. Lippo Lippi was the most profligate of all in his private life, but "his subjects were always religious . . . because his cloistered life procured him countless commissions . . . a proof that the paganism of the Renaissance did not exclude a taste for religious pictures."[40]

---

* Filippo Brunelleschi designed the dome of Florence Cathedral and was a leading sculptor and architect of the Italian Renaissance.

39. A. G. Dickens, *Reformation and Society* (London: Harcourt, Brace & World, Inc., 1966), p. 58.

40. G. G. Coulton, *Art and the Reformation* (Anchor Books, by permission of Cambridge University Press, 1928), p. 428.

Two events which must be considered related to Renaissance humanism are of fundamental importance to Christianity since the sixteenth and seventeenth centuries. In 1522 Martin Luther completed, with the collaboration of the German humanist reformer, Philip Melanchthon, the translation of the Bible from the original Greek into the German vernacular language. Although this was in no way the first translation into the vernacular languages of Europeans, the work of Luther was largely instrumental in making the written Word available to the common people of Germany and thus furthering the Reformation. In 1604 a group of English scholars began a seven-year project in providing a similar vernacular translation for English-speaking people. Whenever we acknowledge the power and importance of the King James Authorized Version of the Bible, we must in all honesty acknowledge some debt to the growth of humanistic scholarship in England.

The Renaissance image of man, equipped with a broad appreciation for an understanding in the classics, in a wide group of interests, and a tolerance for other people, all crowned with a focus on the lordship of Christ and the enlightenment of the Word, provided the foundation for the modern Christian school and Christian education. I consider myself a product of and an admirer of that tradition.

But the Renaissance willingness to make Man an integral being who is able to stand without the redeeming grace of God, who can grow toward personal salvation with no blood of Jesus Christ, and who is unable to say with the publican in Jesus' story, "God, be merciful to me a sinner," lacks the most important dimension of Christian understanding and obedience. Even so, we commit dishonesty and diminish our testimony when we confuse Renaissance humanism with twentieth-century naturalistic humanism. Let us be careful in sorting out the thrust of each so that when we resist Satan we do not do it with our eyes shut.

3

TWENTIETH CENTURY
NATURALISTIC HUMANISM

The previous two chapters represented an attempt to under-score the fact that humanism is not a single entity, a monolithic evil which must be indiscriminately fought by Christians with no regard to what people might mean by the term "humanism." Renaissance humanism, for instance, did tend to exalt Man, but for the most part did not worship him as the central fact of being. God was still held, by most of the humanists of the fifteenth and sixteenth centuries, to be Creator, Lord, and for most Christians, Savior of the human race. Man did increase in his autonomy, and this fact in particular laid the groundwork for an extremely different breed of humanism during the En-lightenment and in the twentieth century.

The terms required to describe twentieth-century naturalistic humanism are many, but as Lamont, a disciple of contemporary humanist thought, acknowledges, most of the terms used now have a great deal in common. The terms *atheistic humanism,* *naturalistic humanism,* or *twentieth-century humanism* usually suggest the same basic doctrine.[1] Even the term *religious humanism* suggests, not the Renaissance acknowledgement of Deity above Mankind, but the kind of humanism which is itself a religion in lieu of traditional religious doctrine which acknowledges a supernatural being.

Lamont criticizes Renaissance humanism and underlines the difference between it and naturalistic humanism by suggesting the theistic difference;

> Brilliant and far-ranging as were the thinkers and writers of the Renaissance, neither Pomponazzi nor better-known Humanist figures like Erasmus and Montaigne, Francis Bacon, and Thomas More, worked out an inclusive metaphysics or theory of the universe that rejected Christian supernaturalism.[2]

Lamont, it would seem, has no claim on most of the writers listed above. Erasmus, for example, was very critical of the established church in his book, *The Praise of Folly,* but never was willing to leave his faith in God and his allegiance to the Catholic Church. He was for a time a friend of Martin Luther but broke with him, not because of Luther's supernaturalism, but because of the *sola fide* doctrine and the Protestant emphasis on the Scriptures over tradition. Thomas More also remained a faithful Roman Catholic for all his humanistic tendencies and eventually lost his life to Henry the Eighth because of his unswerving allegiance to his understanding of Christ and His Church, which More believed to be the Roman Catholic faith.

In keeping with some other twentieth-century humanists, Lamont also breaks with the Renaissance humanists over their enthusiasm for the ancient Greek classics:

---

1. Corliss Lamont, *The Philosophy of Humanism,* 5th Edition (New York: Frederick Unger Publishing Co., 1949 [1977]), Chapter I.
2. *Ibid.,* p. 21.

. . . the academic Humanism founded in the early nineteen-thirties by Irving Babbitt, a Harvard Professor, and Paul Elmer More, an author and editor, emphasized a literary and educational program with supernaturalistic and reactionary tendencies. In philosophy it adhered to a false Dualism of Man versus Nature. And it revived some of the bad features of Renaissance Humanism by setting up a return to the ancient classics as the foundation stone of education and by opposing the Humanities to science.[3]

In order to fully understand the language used by contemporary humanists in their doctrinal statements, it becomes necessary at this point to define a few terms and to describe a few categories used in philosophy which pertain to the humanist world view.

The three categories of philosophy which have dominated human questions about metaphysics for two or three thousand years have related to the questions of *being,* or what is real, of *knowledge* or how does one know anything, and of *values,* or what really matters to us. Very briefly, we shall discuss some of the traditional approaches to these questions.

THE QUESTION OF BEING

Questions about *what is real* have usually included questions about two primary categories: (1) the *stuff of being* or of what the universe consists; and (2) is there meaning and freedom in the universe? Answers to the question about the stuff of the universe have included monistic answers, or the belief that ultimately all being is one kind of thing, and dualistic answers, or the belief that there are basically two kinds of being making up the universe. Idealistic monists believe that ultimately material things are ephemeral and lack true reality, and that ideas alone are basic truth. With this doctrine, concepts such as love, fidelity, and truth are real; but money, houses, and machinery are only real in the sense that they are comprehended by conscious minds

---

3. *Ibid.*

and thus become ideas. For an idealist, not to be known is not to exist at all. We usually associate this concept with the doctrine of Plato, although that philosopher was not a "pure" idealist. Some early Christian doctrines, including those of the Gnostics, were probably related to neo-Platonism or idealism which to some extent infiltrated the Christian Church through Alexandria in Egypt.

The other kind of monism is much more familiar to those who live in the twentieth century and is called *naturalism*. Monistic naturalism holds that the only reality consists of physical or material things. We may use the term *love* in order to communicate, but love only exists in a particular situation where an individual may love another individual or a group. There is no such universal concept as love or truth or faithfulness, but there are individual examples of all of them. Since for the naturalist only material things exist, it is absurd to speak either of love as a universal concept or of things of the Spirit. Beauty, truth, goodness, all have individual examples but cannot be defined in universal terms.

The Judeo-Christian heritage teaches us of a dualistic universe where both material things and ideas have their own existence. This doctrine accepts God's creation in physical terms and the fact that the Word was God. For the dualist, it makes perfectly good sense to speak of the mind or the spirit controlling the physical body and bringing it under subjection. There have been times in the history of Christianity that theologians have tried to deemphasize the physical aspect of Creation, but usually a succeeding generation of Christian thinkers has brought the dualistic acceptance of God's universe back into balance. The Reformation asserted this dualism so strongly that some Counter-Reformation priests felt that the unity of the human person was lost. When mind and body become so polarized that two essential personalities seem to emerge we speak of a person as being pathologically schizophrenic. The New Testament ideal of man underscores a harmony of mind, body, and spirit, but with the spirit and/or mind in control.

The other aspect of the question of being where naturalistic humanism of the twentieth century takes issue with the Judeo-Christian belief is in the area of meaning and determinism in the universe. The question is really one: Is there meaning in the universe, is the universe a hospitable place to live, is anyone in charge here, is justice to be expected at some point, and can an individual life have meaning? The position which answers "yes" to all these questions is called *teleological* and is usually associated with faith in God, or some supernatural being who is the prime mover of the universe. The other question associated with this one is whether we are free, or whether our lives are determined beforehand by either supernatural or natural forces. Extreme religious predestination denied the privilege of choice to an individual; contemporary behaviorism through the person of B. F. Skinner denies that the terms *freedom* and *dignity* have any meaning because we are all what we have been conditioned to be and cannot expect to be rewarded for conforming to that preconditioned and reenforced lifestyle, or punished for confirming what our conditioning has prepared us to be. The question of freedom is another area where the Renaissance humanists who remained with the Catholic Church were critical of the Reformation, particularly of John Calvin and to a lesser extent of Martin Luther.

THE DOCTRINE OF KNOWLEDGE

The doctrine of knowledge, termed *epistemology* by philosophers and sometimes by psychologists, is somewhat parallel to the doctrine of being. For those who assert that ideas are real, there is the possibility of having *universals,* concepts which are true everywhere and always. Universals are employed whenever a person asserts that "it is always right to . . ." anything. For those who believe that there are only physical things in the universe, and that knowing is merely a physical stimulus acting upon a physical brain, knowledge is not the grasping of ideas by a mind but an organic response by one physical thing stimulated by another. A rather recent term for the assertion that sense or physical experience is the only way is *logical positivism,* a common doctrine among naturalistic humanists of the twentieth century.

Judeo-Christian dualists still believe that there is such a thing as mind, that the mind can apprehend physical things and particulars, that through revelation from God we can receive universal truths (for example, that God is love), and that we can learn from sense experience, from deduction and revelation.

THE BASIS OF VALUES

It is in the area of value judgments where the contemporary naturalist most clearly reflects his beliefs about what is real and how one knows. For the monistic naturalist, since there are only particulars and no universals, one can only speak of ethics and morality in a "situational" setting; there are individual examples of morality but one cannot lay down principles which have universal validity. Both moral-ethical and aesthetic values, for the naturalist, have their origin through the senses and the senses' perception of the physical world. Yuri Gagarin, in his notorious comment about his unsuccessful search for God on his orbital flight mission, was using the right tools but merely overlooking the pitiful inadequacy of his application from a scientific viewpoint.

For the dualist, the naturalist's assertion that he has utilized his five senses efficiently and faithfully and has, in the process, been unable to find any evidence that God is or that He speaks, is perhaps analogous to my searching for an FM station on my AM radio and deciding that, since I have heard no FM response, there must not be any. From the Christian dualist's point of view, the naturalistic monistic search is conducted in the wrong medium and is doomed from the beginning to failure. In order to create faith in a non-theistic naturalist mind, one must persuade the seeker to see whether life does not have some other dimensions besides those of sense experience.

Dualists assert that values can be objective, that is, the ethical beliefs and actions which are given from God have universal validity and do not depend upon their local application to be true. Most Christian dualists are ready to say "Amen" to their belief that it is wrong to take human life, that it is wrong to steal, that one should honor his father and mother, and that all of these are true everywhere even though they might have overriding values which would place them in tension on occasion. One of the great inconsistencies of many evangelical Christians is the schizophrenia between insistence upon objectivity of Christian values in ethics and the parallel belief of complete subjectivity in aesthetics. The same preacher who believes that he is obligated to preach objective righteousness in morality often implies that "anything goes" in the music of the church, for instance, or in the careless use of his native language. This is one area where naturalistic humanists find, perhaps with good reason, a wide crack in the Christian door.

SOURCES OF TWENTIETH CENTURY HUMANISM

With this brief overview of the battleground of some of the philosophical turf contested by atheistic humanism and Christian faith, consider a brief history of the development of the statements made by twentieth-century humanists:

Paul Kurtz, explaining that the new humanism is different in kind from previous humanistic statements, prefaces an anthology called *The Humanist Alternative* with this apology:

> The present century has been proclaimed as the Humanist century—the century in which anti-Humanist illusions inherited from previous ages have been seriously questioned and shattered. Humanism has historic roots in human civilization; yet it is

only in recent times that these have begun to bear fruit. Using the powerful critical tools of science and logical analysis, modern man now recognizes that the universe has no special human meaning or purpose and that man is not a special product of creation. Anthropocentrism has at last been laid to rest. Modern man now realizes that he is responsible in large measure for his own destiny. Living on a minor planet on the edge of a small galaxy in a vast universe, man has come to see that he cannot look outside himself for salvation. His future, if he has any, is within his control.[4]

Several assumptions are placed on grand parade in this statement. First is the belief that assumptions contrary to those of Kurtz and other naturalistic humanists have been not only questioned seriously, which is clearly true, but shattered, which is not true at all. Many serious scholars in philosophy, biology, logic, physics, astronomy, and other disciplines have gone on record to express their continued belief in dualism—the fact that there are dimensions of being besides those which are physical. It is characteristic of many humanist statements, as we shall note, that they tend to claim the end of the war without taking issue in the battle at hand. He suggests that humanism has not borne much fruit until recently, a statement hard to accept in the light of Erasmus, Michaelangelo, John Milton, Thomas More, and others listed in the previous chapter on the Renaissance. He asserts that the man of today realizes there is no teleology —"no special human meaning" in the universe, and that man is not a product of creation, both issues on which there is yet a mighty array of credible and competent witnesses to the contrary. He clearly locates the center of his break with Christian humanism of the Renaissance when he proclaims the funeral of what he calls *anthropocentrism,* man's belief in himself as the center of the universe or what the Renaissance Christian humanists

4. Paul Kurtz, Ed., *The Humanist Alternative* (Buffalo, N.Y.: Prometheus Books, 1973), p. 5.

proclaimed as the culmination of God's creative handiwork. The proud image of Man, sometimes overly proud but nevertheless conscious of his own worth, was a trademark of Renaissance art and theology, and proclaimed the belief that Man was created in the Image of God. Finally, Kurtz expresses satisfaction that man looks to himself for salvation, not to anyone outside himself. For anyone interested in twentieth-century history, it is difficult to read these lines without choking on reality.

Lamont believes that Naturalism entered the mainstream of Western thought after the middle of the nineteenth century, perhaps given its principal boost by the publication in 1858 of Charles Darwin's *The Origin of Species*. However, he also believes that the principal revival of Naturalism took place in the United States where its most influential school was at Columbia University with Professors John Dewey and J. E. Woodbridge.[5] Lamont, himself a naturalistic humanist, places Dewey in the center of the American development of naturalistic thinking and his emphasis of the scientific method under the structure of what he believes twentieth-century philosophy should be:

> In my opinion Dewey is the twentieth-century philosopher who so far has best understood modern science and scientific method and who most cogently developed their meaning for philosophy and culture. Throughout he places reliance on experimental intelligence as the most dependable way to solve the problems that face the individual and society. Now intelligence, reason, thought, when most effective, are all nothing more or less than scientific method in operation; and Dewey's most persistent plea is that men should apply that method to every sector of their lives and that the most profound need of our day is to extend scientific thinking from the natural sciences to the broad field of social, economic, and political affairs. His full-fledged Naturalism is, then, a massive philosophic system

---

5. Lamont, p. 36.

which is not only itself based on science, but which also considers the advancement of science in every sphere as the best hope of the human race.[6]

The prime difficulty in this statement, as with numerous high-minded goals contained in the humanist manifestos, is the absence of a method for deciding where science should "advance" the human race or what should be the object of the "best hope" available to them. Science, by definition, is a means but not an end.

Another source for twentieth-century naturalistic humanism is Unitarianism. The Unitarian movement, which insists on the oneness of God, the humanity of Jesus, deemphasizes the Spirit, and thus denies the Theistic Trinity, began in Poland late in the sixteenth century, spread to England during the seventeenth, and in the eighteenth became a force in the United States. In 1825 Unitarians broke away from the Congregational Church and established their own organization.[7] Ralph Waldo Emerson is probably the best-known of the nineteenth century transcendentalists who favored a religious humanism and espoused a unitarian doctrine. The Unitarian movement welcomed people who challenged the existence of a personal God and in many ways laid a foundation for the *Humanist Manifesto* of the early twentieth century.

Lamont further outlines the evolution of Unitarianism into natural humanism:

> In a sermon delivered in 1925 the Reverend John H. Dietrich showed how Unitarianism had naturally laid the basis for Humanism. "Unitarianism," he asserted, "offered opportunity for the enunciation of Humanism by virtue of its underlying spirit of spiritual freedom, by its insistence upon intellectual integrity rather than intellectual uniformity, by its offer of religious

---

6. *Ibid.*, p. 37.
7. *Ibid.*, p. 52.

fellowship to every one of moral purpose without regard to his theological beliefs. But this is not the important thing. The real reason why Unitarianism was the natural soil for the growth of Humanism is the fact that Unitarianism was a revolt against the orthodox Christianity in the interest of the worth and dignity of human nature and the interest of human life."[8]

Other historic influences which have helped shape the twentieth-century humanist outlook would include Deism, the belief in a Deity who created the world but has no transcendental interest in it now (Thomas Jefferson entertained this belief), Freudian analytical psychology which found in the human subconscious many of the motivations driving persons, some aspects of Quakerism which were not very strongly theistic, and certain aspects of the visual and musical arts. During the nineteenth century the American patriot Robert Ingersoll wrote and spoke publicly in support of his humanist credo. His credo in eight lines was this:

> Justice is the only worship.
> Love is the only priest.
> Ignorance is the only slavery.
> Happiness is the only good.
> The time to be happy is now.
> The place to be happy is here.
> The way to be happy is to make others so.
> Wisdom is the science of happiness.[9]

In 1933, a time of economic depression, despondency on the part of many Americans, and the era when perhaps more Americans took an overt socialist position than any other and many even joined the Communist Party, a group of humanists published a *Humanist Manifesto* in the journal called *The New Humanist*.

---

8. *Ibid.*, pp. 53-54.
9. Robert G. Ingersoll, quoted in Christopher Morley (ed.), *Familiar Quotations* (Boston: Little, Brown, 1937), p. 603.

Thirty-four men with backgrounds in universities, journals, and liberal and unitarian churches affixed their signatures to the *Manifesto*. The actual author was Roy Wood Sellars, who in 1973 was still Professor Emeritus at the University of Michigan. Elsewhere Sellars has given his outlook which seemed to require a new direction in American philosophy:

> The Humanist argues that the traditional Christian outlook has been undercut and rendered obsolete by the growth of knowledge about man and his world. He has the positive task of reorientation and of revealing a fresh idea of man's condition and situation in the universe as we are beginning to see it.[10]

Sellars unflinchingly ventures his belief that Judeo-Christian theism is constructed on myth, that this myth is somehow dependent upon both Jewish mythology and Hellenic tradition, and that religion come of age must reject both of these sources in favor of contemporary science. Although he believes that Carl Barth, Emil Brunner, Reinhold Niebuhr and other neo-orthodox theologians have momentarily called Christianity back to relevancy, their movement too was a passing language and is already archaic. In his essay quoted above, he describes the genesis of the *Manifesto*:

> During the 1930's I was invited by a small group of people, teachers and ministers, to give a talk at the University of Chicago on the situation in religion. The outcome was that I was asked to formulate basic principles along humanistic lines. I called my formulation *A Humanist Manifesto*. I sent it back and received suggestions, some of which are incorporated in the *Manifesto*. It was then published with the signatures of many outstanding persons in the religious field, and is now called an historical document. I have found that many do not know of its origin and that is why I give this account.[11]

---

10. Roy Wood Sellars, "The Humanist Outlook" in Paul Kurtz (ed.), *The Humanist Alternative* (Buffalo, N.Y.: Prometheus Books, 1973), pp. 133-134.
11. *Ibid.*

Lloyd L. Morain, current editor of the *Humanist,* journalistic successor of *The New Humanist* which published the original *Manifesto,* claims positive results from the 1933 *Manifesto:*

> That document helped liberate many people from the backwaters of traditional and supranaturalistic religion. It gave to many persons throughout the world a name and focus for their philosophy.[12]

The *Humanist Manifesto* of 1933 contains a preamble and fifteen points. Most of these are incorporated in the new document which was presented in 1973. This *Humanist Manifesto II* was written by Paul Kurtz, then editor of *The Humanist*, Edwin H. Wilson, Roy Fairfield and others who say, "Today it is our conviction that humanism offers an alternative that can serve present-day needs and guide humankind toward the future."[13] With an acknowledgement of rapidly-changing conditions, Editor Morain asks whether it might be time to offer *Humanist Manifesto III*. This new document would be offered on behalf of the American Humanist Association.[14]

With the assumption that the *Humanist Manifesto II* (from here on to be dubbed merely *Manifesto II*) incorporates most of the aspects of philosophy from both documents which are in conflict with historic and revealed Christianity, this critique will be confined to the newer document.

The first section under the general title, *Religion,* contains two basic statements. The first statement expresses a judgment that theistic religion is not only useless but downright harmful:

> We believe . . . that traditional dogmatic or authoritarian religions that place revelation, God, ritual, or creed above human needs and experience do a disservice to the human species. Any

---

12. Lloyd L. Morain, "Humanist Manifesto II—A Time for Reconsideration?" *The Humanist,* September/October 1980, p. 4.

13. *Ibid.*

14. *Ibid.*

account of nature should pass the tests of scientific evidence; in our judgment, the dogmas and myths of traditional religions do not do so. . . . We find insufficient evidence for belief in the existence of a supernatural; it is either meaningless or irrelevant to the question of the survival and fulfillment of the human race. As nontheists, we begin with humans not God, nature not deity.

Any discussion of evidence can, of course, be prefaced by the exclusion of certain types of evidence. As in court cases, the evidence which is excluded may be that which is most important in conviction or exoneration. In the case of *Manifesto II,* the positivistic premise which precludes any evidence other than sense experience is arbitrarily stated before any evidence is considered. Evidence of a spiritual nature is excluded because we know it just does not exist, is not valid, and is not scientific. The circular problem here is the primary one in communicating with contemporary naturalists who are somewhat in the position of saying, "My mind is made up; don't confuse me with facts" (unless they are empirical).

But even from their own perspective, there is naturalistic evidence which has to be disturbing to the open scientific mind. Questions concerning the development of life, the macrocosm of the vast universe, the relativity of time and space as established in Einstein's and later research, and the difficulty of trying to attribute the entire universe to a gaseous theory which itself has to originate somewhere—these and similar questions have caused many thoughtful scientific minds to consider and believe the doctrine of God and His Creation. The sad thing is that the arrogant way in which the *Manifesto* is stated creates the illusion that all the best evidence is in and that matters of theism are no longer open to consideration. This in itself is a failure to live with the attitude of the scientist, who in the true sense remains an observer to whatever evidence may be presented.

The second statement under the *Religion* section of the document is derived from the first.

Promises of immortal salvation or fear of eternal damnation are both illusory and harmful. They distract humans from present concerns, from self-actualization, and from rectifying social injustices. Modern science discredits such historic concepts as the "ghost in the machine" and the "separable soul." Rather, science affirms that the human species is an emergence from natural evolutionary forces. As far as we know, the total personality is a function of the biological organism transacting in a social and cultural context. There is no credible evidence that life survives the death of the body. We continue to exist in our progeny and in the way that our lives have influenced others in our culture.

Many statements on numerous subjects are somewhat carelessly thrown together in this remarkable paragraph. The opening statement which condemns belief in immortality, judgment, and hope for the future is based on the assumption that there is no immortality for human beings, an assumption which follows the one listed above concerning the existence of God. But if humanists are wrong about God's existence, the rest of the house of cards falls on this fact.

When one hears a statement such as "Historians agree that . . ." one tends to cringe. There is no monolithic group of "all historians" or of all "modern science" and to represent that there is a unified theory or belief is to misrepresent scientific scholarship. Science *per se* actually has nothing it can affirm about the human species except facts concerning man's biological nature, where it has made many significant contributions. Science is not interested in or equipped to study immortality as science. Many people practicing science, however, reject the positivistic thesis of naturalistic monism and believe that there are other realms of existence. The rejection of Judeo-Christian dualism is clear in the *Manifesto*; neither psychologists nor other empirical scientists can agree that this rejection is justified. Experience teaches the Christian that both physical things and ideas and spirit exist.

The humanist is in some difficulty here in affirming certain ethical concepts. He has no way to explain ethical concepts because in his rejection of dualism he has rejected the world of ideas and universals. Most of the positive ethical values affirmed by the *Manifesto* are reflections of a hangover Judeo-Christian ethic. The *Manifesto* rejects the theology which produces the ethical ideas, but attempts to retain the ideas.

Perhaps the most blatant rejection of reality comes in the statement which implies that theistic religion has distracted humans from concerns with this world, from self-actualization, and from rectifying social injustices. Although there are of course noteworthy cases where religionists have failed in their duty of helping other people in need to cope with this world, the Second Commandment in terms of Jesus' teaching is primarily involved with just this process. I think it is difficult to suggest with a straight face that progress made in this world in solving human problems, in developing ethical solutions, in creating significant art works from human experience, and in "rectifying social injustices" have had no source in theistic teaching and Christian inspiration.

The next section and the third affirmation relate to morality and ethics:

> We affirm that moral values derive their source from human experience. Ethics is *autonomous* and *situational,* needing no theological or ideological sanction.

The affirmation made here denies the possibility of universals but the next section affirms the universal validity of *reason* and *intelligence* in solving human problems. The use of science, also, must thus be considered a humanist universal, although the statement we just read suggests that each human experience is *situational.* This means that every ethical question has to be considered autonomously, that there are no overruling and abiding principles which one can apply, and yet that we know *a priori* (ahead of time) that science is the proper instrument to analyze the situation. While universals are denied, science is proposed as a universal. The Christian can agree with the humanist that ethics stems from human need and interest, just as the Law of Moses addresses human problems from a divine level. The Lord Jesus Christ began with a human situation on numerous occasions when during His ministry He taught the Christian response. Always, however, he had a principle which was derived from one's acceptance of the sovereignty of God and the Lordship of Christ. One is reminded, among other occasions, of the man born blind, of the woman taken in adultery, of the woman who dared wash Jesus' feet with her hair before His crucifixion, of His concern for the hungry, and of the long list of human situations detailed in the Gospels.

The remaining fourteen items addressed in *Manifesto II* relate derivatively from these three or four. There is an emphasis upon freedom for the individual religiously, politically, intellectually, artistically, and judicially. When one deals with these freedoms the Christian has no basic debate with the aspirations of the humanists. The preciousness of the individual person affirmed by the *Manifesto* is proclaimed more emphatically in the Sermon on the Mount. While condemning puritanical attitudes (which are blamed on religion), the *Manifesto* pleads for responsibility in matters of sexuality. Of course there is no thought at all that sexuality is a gift from a Creator God who along with the gift has provided principles for its responsible use in the generation of human happiness. Separation of church and state, personal equality, universal education, participatory democracy, and the renunciation of force as a means of solving international disputes are areas where the *Manifesto* reflects common concerns with the Christian Church. And the final homily which pleads, "Let us call for an end to terror and hatred" rings a bell of empathy in every Christian heart.

But let us not miss the point which the *Manifesto* makes at the beginning of the document. There is no sense in which this can be considered a Christian document, or one compatible with the Christian cause. The *Manifesto II* underlines the importance of the human situation at the same time it attempts to deprive men and women of the very basis on which they can reasonably regard themselves as important in the universe—that is, the fact that they are created in the Image of God. After sullying that image in sin, they are recreated by the blood of Christ. In these two acts by the Father and the Son, the human race has every reason to walk in joy and aspiration of freedom. When the Creation by God and the Redemption in Jesus are both discarded, all the Manifestos from the beginning of history will not enable us to reestablish Man as anything more than Solomon perceived the humanistic enterprise: "Vanity, vanity, all is vanity, says the preacher."

4

PROBLEMS OF NATURALISTIC HUMANISM

Chapter 3 attempted to provide a critical presentation of the *Humanist Manifesto II* of 1973 with some background of the philosophical and personal considerations which entered into that document. So far in this series we have attempted to underline the thesis that humanisms are not at all one monolithic core of ideas, but that while most humanistic expressions do emphasize the primacy of the study of Man, there is a wide divergence between the classical humanism of the Greeks and Romans, the Christian humanism of the Renaissance, and naturalistic humanism of the twentieth century. Os Guiness in his Christian book, *The Dust of Death,* contends that humanism is a *good* word and needs to be strengthened, but in the context of obedience to God:

> Thus, optimistic humanism is currently in the throes of a
> gathering crisis. But we dare not let this negate the humanness

of its ideals. What is needed is a stronger humanism, not a weaker one. We need a concern for humanness that has a basis for its ideals and the possibility of their substantial realization.[1]

Dr. Francis Shaeffer, Bible scholar and founder of the L'Abri Fellowship in Switzerland, is not this positive about the concept of humanism. He has said, "All roads from Humanism lead to chaos. Humanism is not a builder, it is a destroyer."[2]

Nelson E. Hinman, Pastor of the Church of the Highlands in Burlingame, California and student of psychology, is also somewhat indiscriminating in speaking of humanism—any humanism— as being incompatible with Christianity.[3] Tim LaHaye, in his "Foreword" to Hinman's critical book on humanistic psychology, speaks of humanism as one monolithic entity and calls it "the most destructive force in our society today."[4]

Yet, LaHaye proceeds directly to lament that our "once-great school system" founded on "the Christian consensus, with its roots in the northern European reformation thinking," and its emphasis on "hard work, self-discipline, learning skills, self-sacrifice, and basic morality to achieve self-respect" has been replaced by contemporary emphasis on "sex, self-indulgence, government-supplied necessities, freedom of expression, etc." with its consequent drastic decline in learning skills.[5] The school system LaHaye is holding up as example is one based on the Renaissance humanities as perceived through the German Reformation. In truth, therefore, it is difficult to believe that he is as critical as the rather careless statements in this book would

---

1. Os Guiness, *The Dust of Death* (Downers Grove, Ill.: InterVarsity Press, 1973), p. 38.

2. Quoted in Tim LaHaye, "Foreword" to Nelson E. Hinman, *An Answer to Humanistic Psychology* (Irvine, California: Harvest House Publishers, 1980), p. iii.

3. Hinman, p. 21.

4. LaHaye, p. iii.

5. *Ibid.*

indicate of all humanisms; rather he is focusing his attack primarily on twentieth-century nontheistic naturalistic humanism, the kind which is described in the *Humanist Manifesto II.*

I should like to reiterate my own belief that just as humanists damage their own cause by circular and fuzzy attacks which miss the very stuff of which Christianity consists, so Christians blunt their criticism of atheistic humanism when in their attacks they fail to distinguish the particular doctrines which are inimical to Christian faith. For this reason I should like to reassert my own feeling of the importance of our having some understanding of classic humanism, of Renaissance humanism, and of some of the divergent trends in twentieth-century humanisms. All three of these movements have concepts and results which can be beneficial to the human race, but which can be and often are asserted as alternatives to Christian faith.

This study will include a review of three areas which relate to naturalistic humanism in our time but which are not necessarily based on the same hypothesis. The three widely-divergent areas chosen for this presentation are behavioristic psychology, philosophical existentialism, and technocracy. To focus the contrast between naturalistic humanism and Christianity, consider Nelson Hinman's chart which compares the two doctrines on seven key points:[6]

1. Humanism rejects the Bible as a rule and guide for life's values and behavior. Christianity accepts the Bible as the only rule and guide for life's values and behavior.

2. Humanism denies the existence of a personal God. Christianity rests solidly on the existence of a personal God.

3. Humanism believes that man is competent to solve his life problems without supernatural assistance. Christianity believes that man is wholly unable to solve his basic life problems without God-given assistance.

6. Hinman, p. 21.

4. Humanism teaches that man is autonomous, a law unto himself. Christianity teaches that God is sovereign and that man is obligated to obey Him.

5. Humanism encourages self-exaltation and self-love. Christianity requires self-denial, love of God, and love of one's neighbor.

6. Humanism focuses man's attention on helping himself. Christianity focuses man's attention on helping others.

7. Humanism is totally self-oriented. Christianity is totally Christ-oriented.[6]

BEHAVORISM

Behaviorism in psychology is founded upon the hypothesis that man is controlled by his environment. A prominent contemporary advocate of behaviorism describes the meaning of the term in this way:

> The other way of knowing other than a passive or contemplative way of knowing is a matter of what a person *does*. We can usually observe this as directly as any other phenomenon in the world; no special kind of knowing is needed. We explain why a person behaves as he does by turning to the environment rather than to inner states or activities. The environment was effective during the evolution of the species and we call its result on man the human genetic endowment. A member of the species is exposed to another part of that environment during his lifetime, and from it he acquires a repertoire of behaviour which converts an organism with a genetic endowment into a person. By analyzing these effects of the environment, we move toward the prediction and control of behaviour.[7]

B. F. Skinner, perhaps the best-known contemporary behaviorist, also suggests that his psychological system is not dualistic,

---

6. Hinman, p. 21.
7. B. F. Skinner, "Humanism and Behaviourism" in Paul Kurtz (ed.), *The Humanist Alternative* (Buffalo, N.Y., 1973), p. 98.

such as we have asserted the Judeo-Christian heritage to be, with body and mind as separate entities, but that states of mind and states of bodies are ultimately one and the same. He says:

> A thoroughgoing dualist would say no, because for him what a person observes through introspection and what a physiologist observes with his special techniques are in different universes. But it is a reasonable view that what we feel when we have feelings are states of our own bodies and that the states of mind we perceive through introspection are other varieties of the same kinds of things.[8]

Hinman describes the system in less positive terms than Skinner:

> Behaviorism says that man is a prisoner of his environment, is locked into the machine-like universe in which he lives, and is himself part of that machine, trapped and programmed by it. Behaviorism says that man can be controlled by manipulating his environment. By a reward-and-punishment system, by good or bad primary and secondary reinforcements (which give either pleasure or pain), man can be made to be or do whatever the manipulator wishes.[9]

John Watson, who lived until 1958, was an American physiologist who is sometimes known as the "father of behaviorism." Watson, with other scientific-minded psychologists, despaired of knowing accurately what went on in the minds of their subjects by merely asking them, even by probing the subconscious as Freud and the psychoanalytical psychologists attempted to do. They concluded that the only empirical evidence they could gather about the study of the human mind would be in the arena of human behavior. When the mind and physical behavior were equated, Christian and Biblical dualism were discarded. Hinman puts it dramatically:

---

8. Skinner, p. 99.
9. Hinman, p. 53.

So what started out to be a study of the dualism of man (his nonmaterial nature and his material nature) became a one-dimensional study.[10]

The concept of reenforcement for negative and positive behaviors is a fundamental aspect of behaviorism. A child's environment is seen to include both the natural aspects of his habitat and the negative and positive reenforcement his parents and other individuals give him for specified behaviors. Skinner himself worked with a controlled environment with one of his own children and has worked a great deal with rodents in studying the results of reenforcing mechanisms in behavior. His book, *Beyond Freedom and Dignity,* was probably the best-known publication of any behaviorist psychologist. In this book Skinner reasoned that since each individual is a product of the environmental forces which have made him what he is, that one should not punish people for acting in predictably negative ways or reward others for merely fulfilling the directions which reenforcement earlier in life has made inevitable. Thus one loses the conventional sense of freedom and becomes a product of mechanism, the same criticism which humanists levied at the Reformation with its doctrine of predestination.

Three primary aspects of behaviorism seem to oppose this system directly to Christianity:

1. It is a monistic naturalistic system which has no place for the concept of mind or spirit, but only for a monistic biological organism. It thus denies Biblical dualism.

2. It places the subject at the mercy of the reenforcer who becomes a manipulator. Thus one's freedom is further sacrificed to the values of one who does the manipulating.

3. It denies the freedom of a person and is in a polarized position from the Adam of Genesis who was accorded the freedom to choose his own course.

---

10. *Ibid.,* p. 52.

Behavioristic psychology is not usually regarded as a humanistic approach to persons *per se*. Skinner has debated publicly with humanistic psychologists such as Carl Rogers, and has written critically of Abraham Maslow, another humanistic psychologist. Skinner asserts that behaviorism does serve human needs and provide human functions, and like the humanists of *Manifesto II*, asserts a rather evangelistic urgency for his position.

> Men and women have never faced a greater threat to the future of their species. There is much to be done and done quickly, and nothing less than the active prosecution of a science of behaviour will suffice.[11]

The principal points of contact between behaviorism and naturalistic humanism would include their total emphasis upon scientific method as the only way of human knowing, rejection of traditional Judeo-Christian dependence upon theism, their belief that salvation must come from Man himself, and emphasis upon technology. The primary point of disparity would be between their concepts of freedom. Twentieth-century humanism believes human freedom is possible and asserts the need for its development. Behaviorism acknowledges that we are all products of our environment and that freedom is only a name for something we aspire to but is not a fact of human existence. Behaviorism by its nature is amenable to limited biological engineering of the human species. *Humanist Manifesto II* says, "Although science can account for the causes of behavior, the possibilities of individual *freedom of choice* exist in human life and should be increased."

Hinman summarizes his critique in these words:

> To many psychologists, behaviorism has so dehumanized man that he has ceased to exist as man. In other words, to the pure behaviorist, man exists as a machine or as an animal; he

---

11. Skinner, p. 105.

does not have qualities and traits that differentiate him from an animal or a machine.[12]

Though humanism and behaviorism see themselves at definite odds concerning human nature, they share several fundamental concepts which deny the Bible's theism, its human dualism, and its promise of freedom.

The psalmist comments on almost all of these questions in this compact poem:

> When I look at thy heavens, the work of thy fingers,
>   the moon and the stars which thou hast established;
> What is man that thou art mindful of him,
>   and the son of man that thou dost care for him?
> Yet thou hast made him little less than God,
>   and dost crown him with glory and honor.
> Thou hast given him dominion over the works of thy hands;
>   Thou hast put all things under his feet,
> all sheep and oxen, and also the beasts of the field,
> the birds of the air, and the fish of the sea,
>   whatever passes along the paths of the sea.
> O Lord, our Lord, how majestic is thy name in all the earth![13]

EXISTENTIALISM

Existentialism is a philosophy which began out of a Christian understanding of God and of individual persons. In its emphasis upon the sacredness of individuals, it builds upon the teachings of Jesus. Its beginning as a philosophical system during the nineteenth century is usually associated with the Danish theologian-philosopher Søren Kierkegaard, although some of the doctrines of the anti-theistic German thinker Friedrich Nietzsche tend to surface in some aspects of early Existential thought. Existentialism is based on the German noun, *Existenz,* and emphasizes the

---

12. Hinman, p. 67.
13. Psalms 8 (RSV)

terms, *I exist, I am*. The only relevance for persons is as individuals and they should be respected in that autonomy of time and place. Existentialism tends to diminish the traditional importance ascribed to history and to social institutions. Existential thought tends to be subjective—in fact, Kierkegaard himself once said "Truth . . . is subjectivity."[14]

Mairet, in describing the Danish Kierkegaard's struggle in dealing with the personal intrusions he felt that the nationally-governed Protestant Church in Denmark made on the individual's faith, describes Kierkegaard's thrust:

> For it was in the subjective sphere, in the inward relation of oneself to oneself and to the subjectivity of others, that one became aware of God and of a relation to Him. . . . What was omitted from this development of ideas was the real subject— man, in the total, unfathomable inwardness of his being. Looking back upon that period of thought in the light of its consequences, one can scarcely deny that the protest of Kierkegaard had at least the typical justification for a philosophic rebellion. He spoke up for what was being neglected or ignored.[15]

Anyone who has read with interest the thoughts of the original movers of the American Restoration Movement must have some empathy with some of Kierkegaard's motives. To establish freedom from ecclesiasticism and to establish personal responsibility and priesthood of the individual before God, these are common threads which run through both the early Existential movement and the American Restoration Church. But the individuation required by Kierkegaard almost seems to make impossible the concept of the Church as a body of people. Mairet tells us that Kierkegaard says, at the end of his *Final Postscript,* "the motive that runs through all his writings is the desire 'to read *solo* the

---

14. Philip Mairet, "Introduction" to Jean-Paul Sartre, *Existentialism and Humanism* (Tr. by Philip Mairet) (Brooklyn, N.Y.: Haskell House Publishers, Ltd., 1977), p. 6.

15. *Ibid.,* pp. 6, 7.

original text of the individual human existence relationship, the old text, well-known, handed down from the fathers, to read it through yet once more, if possible, in a more heartfelt way.' "[16]

Ralph Wilburn, writing on "Disciple Thought in Protestant Perspective," notes the tension between individualism and community which occurs in church congregations:

> These, then, are two evils in church polity to be avoided: (1) *the kind* of congregationalism which loses the values of organic oneness in true catholicity, and (2) *the kind* of catholicity which eradicates the evangelical principle of "the free congregation of the free Word of God," as Karl Barth expresses it. Both evils represent distortions in the historical actualization of the church.[17]

Kierkegaard's successors divided into both theistic and nontheistic circles. One of the interesting things about existentialism is the fact that the attitude toward theism has not seemed to keep the groups separate. On the nontheistic side Heidigger and Jean-Paul Sartre are the best-known names; on the theistic side the name of Karl Jaspers is probably the most widely read.

Sartre's existentialism is known chiefly through his literary and dramatic works. The play, *No Exit,* which describes the existential situation of persons to the level of near absurdity, is probably the best known document of existential literature. Sartre, however, did write an apology for existentialism called *Existentialism and Humanism.*[18] Although some humanists and some existentialists would deny the close relationship of the movements, Sartre himself recognizes the fact that the high level

---

16. *Ibid.*, p. 8.

17. Ralph G. Wilburn, "Disciple Thought in Protestant Perspective: an Interpretation," in Ralph Wilburn (Ed.), *The Reconstruction of Theology* (St. Louis: Bethany Press, 1963), p. 327.

18. Jean-Paul Sartre, *Existentialism and Humanism* (Brooklyn, N.Y.: Haskell House Publishers, Ltd., 1977).

of individualization and autonomy demanded by his philosophy tends to elevate man to a central point in existence. He explains:

> Many may be surprised at the mention of humanism in this connection, but we shall try to see in what sense we understand it. In any case, we can begin by saying that existentialism, in our sense of the word, is a doctrine that does render human life possible; a doctrine, also, which affirms that every truth and every action imply both an environment and a human subjectivity.[19]

The relationship of this doctrine with the *Humanist Manifesto II* is a little clearer when one considers Point Five: "We believe in maximum individual autonomy consonant with social responsibility." And Sartre provides the key to the relationship:

> Aesthetic existentialism, of which I am a representative, declares with greater consistency that if God does not exist there is at least one being whose existence comes before its essence, a being which exists before it can be defined by any conception of it. That being is man or, as Heidigger has it, the human reality. What do we mean by saying that existence precedes essence? We mean that man first of all exists, encounters himself, surges up in the world—and defines himself afterwards. . . . There is no human nature, because there is no God to have a conception of it. Man simply is. . . . Man is nothing else but that which he makes of himself. That is the first principle of existentialism.[20]

The logical extension of existentialism to its own ultimate fulfillment leads to absurdity. That is to say, that when the ties which bind individuals to each other, to history, and to institutions, and most of all to God are severed, the very cause-effect relationship upon which both science and common sense depend is lost too. Christianity emphasizes the importance of the individual and the Bible speaks of the preciousness of human life

---

19. Sartre, *Op. Cit.,* p. 24.
20. *Ibid.,* pp. 27-28.

in both Testaments. But Biblical theology holds individualism and personal relationships in creative tension. "For freedom hath Christ set us free," trumpets St. Paul in the letter to the Galatians, and again the apostle asks the Corinthians, "Why should my liberty be determined by another man's scruples?"[21] But in the spirit of being my "brother's keeper" from the first book of the Bible, Paul emphasizes, "Let no one seek his own good, but the good of his neighbor."[22] And the triangle of self, neighbor, and God is complete late in the same chapter when he says, "So, whether you eat or drink, or whatever you do, do all to the glory of God. Give no offense to Jews or to Greeks or to the church of God, just as I try to please all men in everything I do, not seeking my own advantage, but that of many, that they may be saved."[23]

Humanism is also in tension with existentialism because the open embrace of pure existential doctrine would endanger the scientific spirit of experiment, cause and effect upon which the framers of *Manifesto II* were so insistent. Yet, existentialism remains one of the strongest statements of humanism in the twentieth century and it is impossible for humanists, any more than for Christians, to ignore the movement.

Alienation and a certain strain of deep pessimism have pervaded the existential philosophy. In one sense, this has provided a needed check for the easy optimism of naturalistic humanism with its utopian dream of a better humanistic world around the next corner. Sometimes, however, it has led to the depths of despair. Jean-Paul Sartre has said, "Let us look at ourselves if we can bear to, and see what is becoming to us. First we must face that unexpected revelation, the striptease of our humanism."[24]

---

21. I Corinthians 10:29b (RSV).
22. *Ibid.*, 10:24.
23. *Ibid.*, 10:31-33.
24. Quoted in Guiness, p. 13.

During the student revolt of the 1960's when students expressed the desire to disassociate themselves from the values and mistakes of their parents and their forefathers, the concept of existentialism was often mentioned as a justification for the existing alienation between generations. Guiness explains the spiritual base for this generation gap:

> Whenever a man is not fulfilled by his own view of himself, his society or his environment, then he is at odds with himself and feels estranged, alienated and called in question.[25]

Various aspects of contemporary art underline the existential predicament. John Cage, whose use of silence to represent a composition for piano, or utter chance in the choice of notes and phrases in musical composition, or the throwing of spitballs at an audience to represent a "happening" in the visual arts, has been a leader of the movement. Samuel Beckett, in his play *Waiting for Godot,* underlines his belief that Godot's failure to arrive at all reduces all of life to "the level of irrational absurdity."[26]

The problems of alienation emanating from existentialism give us pause. It would seem that the absolute Restorationist concept which, like the student existentialists of the 1960's, attempted to ignore history in its belief that it had nothing to do with that history, is an exercise in losing a hold on reality. There is nothing wrong with the intense desire to live by the original documents of the Christian religion. In doing this, however, we cannot ignore that we are also products of the history which has taken place between Jesus and the apostles at the beginning and ourselves at the other end.

Guiness summarizes in one pithy statement the tragedy of existential humanism:

---

25. *Ibid.,* p. 25.
26. *Ibid.,* p. 26.

This alienation, metaphysical and environmental, is an inescapable consequence of humanism and symptomatic of its lack of a basis, making man unfulfillable on the basis of his own views of himself.[27]

Jesus' antidote for existential alienation is the clearest statement I can find: "Thou shalt love the Lord thy God with all thy heart and with all thy soul and with all thy mind; and thou shalt love thy neighbor as thyself."

TECHNOCRACY

The third twentieth-century philosophy which has established itself essentially as a religion, or as a substitute for religion, is what will here be called *technocracy*. The machine itself, of course, like any other of God's gifts, is a neutral quantity which may be used for the development of the Kingdom of God or the kingdom of Satan. The concern expressed here is the elevation of technology from the role of human servant to a way of life which dominates persons and eventually requires their obedience and essentially their worship.

It may be that Americans have historically been somewhat more vulnerable to the claims of the machine age than Europeans or people from the Third World. The American love affair with the automobile, public communications media, and mass production are only latter-day manifestations of a spirit which has resided in the peoples' consciousness for a long time.

At the American Centennial held in Philadelphia in 1876, there were of course exhibitions of art works and architectural designs and other conventional demonstrations of American creativity for the world to review. John A. Kouwenhoven, however, reports on the surprising star of the exhibition which turned out not to be the latest trends in American art, but the great Corliss steam engine which was the "largest and most

---

27. *Ibid.,* pp. 27-28.

powerful engine that had ever been built up to that time." The machine was installed to provide power for the "lathes, grinders, drills, weaving machines, printing presses, and other machinery displayed by the various exhibitors. It weighed altogether 1,700,000 pounds, yet so perfectly was it made that it worked almost as quietly and with as little vibration as a watch."[28]

> People said all the fine things that duty required about the pictures and status in Memorial Hall, but in the presence of the Corliss engine they were exalted. It stood there at the center of the twelve-acre building, towering forty feet above its platform, not an idealization but an unmitigated fact. Yet to the thousands who saw it, it was more than merely the motive power for the miles of shafting which belted their energy to machines throughout the building.[29]

Kouwenhoven comments on some of the artistic tributes to the engine of Philadelphia's American Centennial:

> Consciously or unconsciously, each visitor in his own way testified to its aesthetic impact. Sixty years later the Midwestern poet, Harriet Monroe, remembered being taken from Chicago to Philadelphia to visit the Centennial and recorded that she, at sixteen, was far more impressed by the Corliss engine "turning its great wheels massively" than by any of the art exhibitions. . . . And the French sculptor Bartholdi* said in an official report to his government that the engine had "the beauty and almost the grace of the human form." . . . Even the Brahminic *Atlantic Monthly* concluded rhetorically that "surely here, and not in literature, science, or art, is the true evidence of man's creative powers; here is Prometheus unbound."[30]

It is not the machine as servant, in its ability to do the work of men—even in the robot in an automotive factory which may

---

28. John A. Kouwenhoven, *The Arts in Modern American Civilization* (New York: W. W. Norton Co., Inc., 1948), p. 24.

29. *Ibid.,* pp. 25-26.

* Bartholdi was the sculptor-designer of the Statue of Liberty.

30. *Ibid.,* p. 25.

replace several workers—and it is not the sense of aesthetic appreciation which may admire the grace of a great engine or a beautiful automobile or airplane, but it is the thing-in-itself power of the mechanization, the engineering to replace human values and goals, which challenges the Christian faith in the twentieth century. Even the humanism which was described early in this book and in the previous chapter perceives technocracy as an enemy of personality and human individualism. From the point of view of Christian criticism, however, both humanism and technocracy occupy a similar position of challenge and assume a position which is not acceptable intellectually.

The Christian critique of technocracy, or applied scientism, must include the drive to conformity to an image created by mass media and enforced by peer pressure. It also must resist the tendency to value persons, things, and ideas with the pragmatic criterion which ends with the question, "Does it work?" And finally, Christian thought must contend earnestly for the freedom of the will, the mind, the hopes of a person, and for the individual himself. In this arena, of course, the existentialist sees himself as a willing ally, but unfortunately one who in his pessimistic alienation shuts his eyes to the realities of the natural world which must be faced by all persons, whether they be Christians or existentialists or humanists or technologists.

Jacques Ellul, a French resistance fighter of World War II, was a professor of law in the University of Bordeaux. Ellul has summarized some of the philosophical problems of technocracy as well as anyone in the twentieth century. Os Guiness provides this summary:

> For Jacques Ellul the essence of "technique" is not that it is "mechanical"; rather "technique" is the more subtle "mentality" that grew from the "mechanical." The "mechanical" is merely the crude clockwork of machinery; "technique" is the consciousness of a mechanism applying itself to all man's life and

finally to man himself. It is a principle made out of a process, a mentality made out of a machine, whereby one uses an ensemble of procedures, practices and resources to achieve certain ends. The total aggregate of the best possible means in every field will together produce a technical civilization, covering all man's acts, from shaving to landing on the moon. "Today no human activity escapes this technical imperative," he writes. "Our civilisation is first and foremost a civilisation of means." This technique will be increasingly applied to man in medicine, genetics, education, vocational guidance, advertising and psychology until finally "here man himself becomes the object of technique."[31]

Ellul describes certain features basic to technique. First is the relationship of technique to rationalism. "Technique is the calculus of efficiency, the reduction of facts, figures, forces, and even men to procedures in the service of the tyranny of objective rationalism."[32] The social necessity of the individual's conforming to the rationalistic efficiency of his group is reminiscent of what we have earlier considered the Prussian discipline of the military transferred to all people in society.

The second feature of technique for Ellul is the element of artificiality. Guiness summarizes, "Technique rapidly approaches the point where the natural environment will be replaced by the technological. Some . . . may applaud and welcome this, but most are ill at ease with the plastic unnaturalness of such a world."[33]

A story circulating recently illustrates this contemporary artificiality. A mother in a supermarket is complimented on the appearance of her beautiful little girl. "Thank you, she is pretty," is the proud mother's response, "But you should see her picture!" Franz Kafka, the novelist, once said, "The conveyor's belt of life carries you on, no one knows where. One is more of an object,

---

31. Guiness, p. 132.
32. Guiness, p. 133.
33. *Ibid.*

a thing, than a living creature."[34] A practical example of this principle is provided in a memo of R. K. Price, a speech writer for Richard Nixon in the 1968 election: We have to be very clear on this point that the response is to the image not to the man. . . . It's not what's *there* that counts, it's what's projected —and carrying it one step further, it's not what *he* projects but rather what the voter receives. It's not the man we have to change, but rather the received impression. And this impression often depends more on the medium and its use than it does on the candidate himself."[35]

Albert Speer, Minister of Armaments during the latter days of the Third Reich who served his twenty-year sentence imposed by the Nuremberg Trials in the prison at Spandau, comments on the technocratic evil of the Nazi regime and its perpetual danger:

> In my area, armaments, man had also been devalued, into a production factor. He was as countable as the production figures for tanks, steel, or munitions. Today, moral sensibilities are being suppressed everywhere and the human factor is being ubiquitously degraded by technology. But in the totalitarian state, man was reduced to a commodity or a number in an extreme fashion. The fates of all men, whether Jews or non-Jews, were decided at desks in the interest of armaments and defense.

> Such ethical hardening still exists today, beyond any ideology, regardless of any specific regime, in both bureaucracy and technocracy. Obsessed with performance goals, devoured by personal ambition, people still tend to see human events in the technocratic terms of efficiency. This fundamental problem exists unchanged in our achievement society. Except that the

---

34. David Riesman, *The Lonely Crowd* (New Haven: Yale University Press), p. 123.
35. Quoted in Guiness, p. 125.

situation of war and dictatorship intensified the phenomenon to the extreme.[36]

Aldous Huxley in his *Brave New World* and George Orwell in his equally chilling novel, *1984,* both describe worlds of mechanistic manipulation by leaders of the common people through technology. Possibilities suggested both in the fictional literature and in scientific prognosis for the future include manipulation of the human mind by electronic and other mechanical media (we are already quite familiar with the concept of brainwashing), alteration of beliefs and values by mechanistic means, genetic engineering (control of certain aspects of future generations by biological engineering), monitoring, observation and control of human behavior by electronic means, transfer of monetary funds by electronic rather than paper money means, and scientific manipulation of societal structures through psychological and mechanistic control. The popular movie, *The Boys from Brazil,* reminded its audience that if human cloning becomes a reality, we might see not only reproduced Einsteins, Picassos, and Woodrow Wilsons, but Hitlers and Stalins as well.

Edwin F. Taylor wrote in a 1960 article about the neutrality which science and technology are supposed to have upon ethical and aesthetic values:

> If science is like a tool, then like a tool it has no built-in conscience. Just as a hammer may be used either for building houses or for breaking windows, in the same way science may be used for destructive or constructive purposes. This point does not need to be labored in a world threatened by nuclear holocaust.

> Some of the questions which we consider to be the most important cannot be asked, much less answered, in a scientific context. One such question is, "How should the results of science be used?" As an operational question this is meaningless. No

---

36. Albert Speer, *Infiltration*, tr. by Joachim Neugroschel (N.Y.: Macmillan Publishing Co., Inc., 1981), p. 8.

conceivable physical experiment can give us an answer to it. Yet at the very least the survival of civilization depends upon its answer.[37]

The danger of technocracy to both Christians and to a free society is that science and technology, neutral tools, can be made into values in themselves. When it becomes incumbent upon all people to live in accordance with principles derived from biological evolution or engineering, sociological planning for the future person, family, and society, military efficiency, and a society governed by the pragmatic "Does it work? If so it's good" of Big Business, then technology becomes technocracy. This is the point at which technocracy and naturalistic humanism come together: the assertion that science and technology should be used not only to *attain* human goals but to *ascertain* what those goals ought to be.

People familiar with the Book of Revelation are already aware of the technology outlined in Chapter Thirteen which will be part of the equipment of the future world ruler, the "beast." A recent article by Frank Goines includes an interview between Gary Randall and Ron Steele, a scientist-author. Goines outlines his discovery of a new laser machine in this discussion:

> The hand scan machine is something I just now found out about after seven years of investigating on faith that a Bible prophecy which I heard in 1973 about the mark of the beast where no man will be able to buy or sell unless he has the mark on his right hand or his forehead. . . . I visualized this concept because of my background in electronics and because I was working in computers. When this verse was shown to me from the Bible I could see how all of this could come to pass. I set out at that time trying to track down whether or not it was feasible; if there was a willingness in the banking industry to

---

37. Edwin F. Taylor, "The Limits of Scientific Knowledge," *The Christian Scholar* XLIII/2, Summer 1960, p. 115.

make it possible, and if so what were they doing about it. And also if the hardware was here. Just yesterday I received in the mail from the hand scan company, the machine that is going to read a person's hand with their number.[38]

Whether or not this laser machine which can implant an electronic number into a person's body is the future type of equipment to be used during the Great Tribulation, it is a reminder to us now that in the Name of Christ we need to assert our individual freedom from technocracy and its control over our families, our selves, our own thinking, and to the extent we have influence, over our society and our government.

Again, naturalistic humanism and what has been called technocracy in this paper are to some extent avowed opponents. From one perspective, both end up dealing with human personality by denying the true basis of man's possible greatness—the Image of God in which he is created, the Life of Jesus in which he is redeemed, and the indwelling Spirit in Whom he finds power.

The previous chapter discussed naturalistic humanism, which has maintained an optimistic view of man's future at the cost of ignoring some of the realities about man's nature and his condition. This chapter then outlined some of the propositions of existentialism, a philosophy which contains some strong Christian sentiments, but which in denying much of history and emphasizing the individual's autonomy unduly ends up in personal alienation and inevitable pessimism. Finally we have mentioned technocracy, which takes the useful tools of our age and by using them as gods and masters, makes mankind a slave to his own creation. In this we have gone full circle since Isaiah summarized the problem of his own people long ago: "Their land is filled with idols; they bow down to the work of their hands, to what their own fingers have made."[39]

---

38. Frank Goines, *Prophecy and Economics* 3:2, Feb. 17, 1981.
39. Isa. 2:8 (RSV). See Hab. 2:18-20.

Jesus once said, "Of how much more value is a man than the birds!" (Luke 12:24). Extending this over all creation, He could have said, "Of how much more value is a person than the humanities, than human philosophy, or all the science and technology which can ever be produced!"

Man is "a little lower than the angels." Let us be challenged to use the intelligence, the resources, the material, and the love which God has given us, and to live in the freedom which the redemption of His own Son has accomplished.

5

THE CHRISTIAN IMAGE OF MAN

When I look at thy heavens,
  the work of thy fingers,
the moon and the stars
  which thou hast established;
what is man that thou art mindful of him,
  and the son of man that thou dost care for him?
Yet thou hast made him little less than God,
  and dost crown him with glory and honor.
Thou hast given him dominion over the works of thy hands;
  thou hast put all things under his feet,
all sheep and oxen,
  and also the beasts of the field,
the birds of the air, and the fish of the sea,
  whatever passes along the paths of the sea.
O Lord, our Lord,
  how majestic is thy name in all the earth![1]

1. Ps. 8:3-9 (RSV).

The Book of Genesis introduces three concepts concerning man which are basic to the Christian doctrine of persons, but which themselves have been battleground for differing groups of theologians. These concepts are the creation itself, the *Imago Dei* (Image of God) doctrine, and the meaning of the fall. Each of these will be considered a little more specifically in the light of their sharp differences with the doctrines of secular or naturalistic humanism.

CREATION

The claim of man's creation by direct action of God places Biblical doctrine in direct opposition to a secular humanism such as that expressed in *Manifesto II,* but does not provide material for a break with Renaissance humanism. The creation becomes the basis for man's entire stance as the highest of God's creatures in the universe, for his peculiar relationship with God, for God's caring for all people as sons and daughters (in a limited sense even before redemption through Christ), and for the concept of redemption or restoration through Jesus Christ. Creation is the basis for Man's original praise to God, as in Psalms 33:6-9:

> By the word of the Lord the heavens were made,
> and all their host by the breath of his mouth.
> He gathered the waters of the sea as in a bottle;
> he puts the deeps in storehouses.
>
> Let all the earth fear the Lord,
> let all the inhabitants of the world stand in awe of him!
> For he spoke, and it came to be;
> he commanded, and it stood forth.

The doctrine of creation places Man at the apex of creation, but definitely as *part of it.* Thus his biological nature is dependent upon the same creative origin as other biological beings; in fact, he is properly part of the created universe and of the world. The breath of God which gave him life, however (Gen. 2:7), speaks of a spiritual life which separates him from the other animals and removes him from continuity with their creation. Thus the concept of dualism which has been part of the Judeo-Christian philosophy of being begins with Adam and continues strongly in the New Testament letters of St. Paul, finding a particularly strong modern reaffirmation in the Protestant Reformation.

Paul wrote to the Romans that the creation provides one of the clear reasons for faith in God and His Son: "Ever since the creation of the world his invisible nature, namely, his eternal power and deity, has been clearly perceived in the things that have been made."[2] And the psalmist finds in the created world abundant reason for believing in and glorifying the Creator:

> The heavens are telling the glory of God;
>   and the firmament proclaims his handiwork.
> Day to day pours forth speech,
>   and night to night declares knowledge.
> There is no speech, nor are there words;
>   their voice is not heard;
> yet their voice goes out through all the earth,
>   and their words to the end of the world.[3]

Job's contention with God, and his specific complaint that he had no umpire to stand between him and God, is silenced when he is reminded of the power and the magnificence of God's creative work: "I had heard of thee by the hearing of the ear, but now my eye sees thee; therefore I despise myself, and repent in dust and ashes."[4]

Secular humanism fails to find either the convincing voice of God or sufficient reason for repentance in the universe. Thus, the *Manifesto II* asserts, "We find insufficient evidence for belief

---

2. Romans 2:20a (RSV).
3. Ps. 19:1-4a (RSV).
4. Job 42:5-6 (RSV).

in the existence of a supernatural; it is either meaningless or irrelevant to the question of the survival and fulfillment of the human race. As nontheists, we begin with humans not God, nature not deity."[5]

Humanism generally accepts the concept of both biological and social evolution; in its avoidance of the broader reality of suffering, violence, retrograde human behavior and moral depravity it retains its superficial optimism which summarizes its religious thrust in the words, "No deity will save us; we must save ourselves."[6]

IMAGO DEI

The specific aspect of Creation which has excited the imagination of Christian philosophers about man, however, is the concept of *Imago Dei*. The relationship of this image of God to the fall upon the disobedience of Eve and Adam has been the subject of many volumes of speculation and study. For example, of what did the image of God consist: physical relationship, intellect, spirituality, eternal destiny, or what? And did the fall completely obliterate the original image, pending the redemption of an individual by Christ? What is the state of fallen man in relation to the image of God? A great deal depends upon the answer to *this* question, including questions such as the validity of Christians' following political leaders who are not redeemed, the implied necessity of deciding who is among the redeemed before deciding what voices in the world to hear, and the question of the value of art, music and literature composed by men and women who were not themselves Christians. Recently the question about God's hearing the prayers of Jewish people without Christ was raised in a public way by an official of a major American Protestant denomination. Probably some of these

---

5. *Manifesto II*: "Religion"
6. *Manifesto II*: "Religion"

questions are unanswerable and it might be contended that they don't require answers for simple Christian obedience. It would seem that, in terms of Christians' relationships with non-Christians, they deserve at least serious consideration.

Historically, the concept of the *Imago Dei* has long been interpreted in terms of intellect and rationality. Saint Augustine suggests this interpretation:

> If the soul is therefore called immortal, because it never ceases to live with some life or other, even when it is most miserable, so . . . the human soul is never anything save rational or intellectual; and hence, if it is made after the image of God in respect to this, that it is able to use reason and intellect in order to understand and behold God, then from the moment when that nature so marvellous and great began to be, whether this image be so worn out as to be almost none at all, or whether it be obscure or defaced, or bright or beautiful, certainly it always is.[7]

This interpretation allows for the divine image to be present, though "worn out," obscure or defaced, in all men and probably is at the root of the folk saying that there has to be good in the worst of men. Babbage points out that the same view was held in the Reformation. Calvin wrote:

> This term denotes the integrity which Adam possessed, when he was endued with a right understanding when he had affections regulated by reason, and all his senses governed in proper order, and when in the excellence of his nature he truly resembled the excellence of his Creator.[8]

Merrill F. Unger agrees that the *Imago* is retained in fallen man to some lesser degree, but that

---

7. Augustine, *De Trinitate,* xiv. 4., quoted in Babbage, *Man in Nature and in Grace* (Grand Rapids: Wm. B. Eerdmans Publishing Co., 1957), p. 14.
8. Calvin, *The Institutes of the Christian Religion,* I, 15,3., quoted in Babbage, pp. 14-15.

As to what constituted this image originally, and as to what it still constitutes, it should be said that a too frequent mistake has been to concentrate attention upon some single feature instead of comprehending all those excellent characteristics which, according to the Scriptures, belonged, or belong, to man, and which constitute his likeness to his Maker. Also the effort has been made to distinguish too sharply between that in the likeness which has been lost through sin and that which is permanent.[9]

Genesis 9:6 would seem to sustain the concept that the image is not entirely lost in fallen man, for *after* the fall God says: "Whoever sheds the blood of man, by man shall his blood be shed; for God made man in his own image." James provides a New Testament reminder that we are not to use our tongues for cursing: "With it (the tongue) we bless the Lord and Father, and with it we curse men, who are made in the likeness of God."[10]

John Calvin reiterated his view that the *Imago* consists of the rationality and understanding:

> To condemn the understanding to perpetual blindness so as to leave it to intelligence in any thing, is repugnant, not only to the divine word, but also to the experience of common sense. . . . The human mind, fallen as it is, and corrupted from its integrity, is yet invested and adorned by God with excellent talents.[11]

The Renaissance view of man as interpreted by the Christian humanists of the fifteenth and sixteenth centuries might generally have supported the Calvinistic approach to the image of God. With their heavy emphasis on rationality and wisdom, an emphasis which drove them back to the classics and to the Greek humanists as sources, they appreciated deeply the rational side of God's

---

9. Merrill F. Unger, "Image of God" in *Unger's Bible Dictionary* (Chicago: Moody Press, 1957), p. 516.

10. James 3:9 (RSV).

11. Calvin, *Op. Cit.,* II quoted in Babbage, pp. 15-16.

gift to man and glorified this rationality through their art. Rationality to the Renaissance humanists was generally regarded as a gift from God and not an autonomous quality as is held by the authors of *Humanist Manifestos I* and *II*.

Babbage questions, however, whether the gift of rationality and understanding is really what the image of God is all about.

> Man, created by God, is placed in the Garden, and commanded to "dress it and to keep it" (Gen. 2:15). He is given power and authority over the beasts of the field, but he is solemnly forbidden to eat "of the tree of the knowledge of good and evil" (Gen. 2:17). Man's powers, according to the Biblical revelation, are conferred and bestowed: they are neither absolute nor original. Man's relation to God is one of creaturely dependence, in which he enjoys delegated authority; and, as a created being, he is called to live in trust and obedience. He is called to respond to fatherly goodness with filial trust: to grace with faith. Consequently, he is called to recognize and confess that the true center of his life is not within himself but beyond himself. The Biblical story is the record of the destruction of this relationship by willful self-assertion and rebellion. The result is man's undoing, and the experience of God's love as wrath.[12]

This concept of the *Imago Dei* does place man squarely at the opposite end of the pole from which twentieth-century naturalistic humanism tries to place him: the Image suggests man's utter dependence and delegated authority only; naturalistic humanism insists on man's autonomous personality and his responsibility of working out his own salvation without any dependence on any other being, theistic or natural. From the Biblical point of view, this is exactly the point where the *Manifesto* asserts its most aggressive arrogance and thus from the Christian's point of view, even blasphemy. This is also the point, however, where most Christians find the greatest difficulty in following

---

12. Babbage, p. 16.

Jesus Christ: it is difficult for human beings to let go and say with St. Paul, "It is no longer I who live, but Christ who lives in me."[13]

From this orientation, Jesus fulfilled completely the image of the Godhead when He was able to pray in Gethsemane, "Not as I will, but as thou wilt."[14] In this, Jesus denied autonomy from the Father, rebuked the Satanic temptation for intellectual and personal independence offered in the Garden of Eden, and revealed fully the *Imago Dei* suggested in Genesis: "Let us make man in our image." Here Jesus became fully the Son of Man while He sustained His relationship as the Son of God.

Babbage develops this point of view further in his book, *Man in Nature and in Grace*:

> Thus the *Imago Dei* is not a doctrine about man's being in himself; it is rather an acknowledgement that he depends entirely upon the will of another. The *analogia entis* is replaced by the *analogia actus,* since man is only what he is by virtue of the relation in which he stands to God.[15]

Although I believe Babbage is partially correct in seeing the fall and the surrender to temptation by Adam and Eve as a bid for autonomy and independence, I do not believe the scriptures sustain the belief that all of the image was lost in man's fall and his grasping for personal and intellectual independence. The passages quoted above suggest that after the fall, both in the Old Testament and the New, there was in all men a replication of God's image which made their persons and their bodies sacred. To this extent, it seems to me that we have a fellowship with the Christians of the fifteenth and sixteenth centuries who asserted the sacredness of human beings because of man's being created by God.

---

13. Galatians 2:20b (RSV).
14. Matthew 26:39c (RSV).
15. Babbage, pp. 16-17.

There is another point of view about the image which relates to the physical body. This position is defended by the appearance of Jesus in a visible body after His resurrection, His partaking of food in fellowship with His disciples, and the empirical claim of the apostle John to being a qualified witness: "That which was from the beginning, which we have heard, which we have seen with our eyes, which we have looked upon and touched with our hands, concerning the word of life—the life was made manifest, and we saw it, and testify to it, and proclaim to you the eternal life which was with the Father and was manifest to us—that which we have seen and heard we proclaim also to you, so that you may have fellowship with us."[16] John's claim to sense experience in his witness of Christ's resurrection would qualify him as a witness in an American court of law, and it is an interesting study to note the long list in a major concordance of the Bible under the word "witness" in the New Testament.

It is apparent that the Spirit in giving the New Testament intended for the Word of Scripture to stand on the testimony of its witnesses, and these witnesses did claim an empirical experience with the risen Lord. Faith, ultimately, is placed in the testimony of the witness and not in the personal feeling of the believer, and for this reason it seems important that the concept of the *Imago Dei* in a physical sense not be discarded too quickly. Paul is concerned that the mortal *put on* immortality and that the corruptible *put on* the incorruptible, but he does not suggest the immortal annihilation of that which is natural and physical. Problems arise here, of course, in dealing with the natural problems of living in our bodies: injury, and such problems seem difficult to reconcile with the image-of-God concept in relation to our biological origins. I do not believe that this is the most important aspect of our being created in God's image or of our redemption in Christ, but I do note that Paul is concerned that our bodies be "God's temple" and treated with the

16. I John 1:1-3a (RSV).

reverence due such a temple.[17] "Glorify God in your body," Paul admonishes the Corinthians, and it would seem to me that he speaks of our remembering in whose image we are made.[18]

The Renaissance humanists, of course, accepted this aspect of the *Imago* with joy. The sculpture, portraiture, and glorying in the classical image of man, which was preserved in the dynamic and proud busts of athletic Greeks, served as models for some of the sculpture of the prophets, the saints, and the angels. Again, in my judgment, their emphasis was out of balance, but they did uphold one aspect of scriptural truth about God's intent for man.

THE FALL

What then was the Fall? The word as such is not a Biblical one, but it seems descriptive of the history recorded in Genesis Chapter 3. Man, created in a state of moral purity but also in a state of complete moral freedom, was subjected to temptation from a source outside himself. The temptation came in the form "of an appeal to both man's intellect and to the senses. The forbidden fruit was presented as 'good for food' and 'to be desired to make one wise.' Thus the allurement was in the direction of sensual gratification and intellectual pride."[19]

Both these rebellions against God and the ethical system He gives are clearly evident in *Manifesto II* of naturalistic humanism.

> *Reason and intelligence* are the most effective instruments that humankind possesses. There is no substitute: neither faith nor passion suffices in itself. . . . Yet critical intelligence, infused by a sense of human caring, is the best method that humanity has for resolving problems.[20]

---

17. I Cor. 3:16-17; 6:16-20 (RSV).
18. *Ibid.*
19. Unger, "Fall of Man," *Op. Cit.,* p. 342.
20. *Manifesto II,* "Ethics."

92

In terms of sensuality, the *Manifesto* speaks specifically only of the area of sexuality:

> In the area of sexuality, we believe that intolerant attitudes, often cultivated by orthodox religions and puritanical cultures, unduly repress sexual conduct. While we do not approve of exploitive, denigrating forms of sexual expression, neither do we wish to prohibit, by law or social sanction, sexual behavior between consenting adults. The many varieties of sexual exploration should not in themselves be considered "evil." . . . Short of harming others or compelling them to do likewise, individuals should be permitted to express their life-styles as they desire.[21]

Christians, of course, do not take issue with all the attitudes about sexuality or numerous other issues raised by the *Manifesto*. Many of the values are vestigial Christian ideals borrowed by humanism without crediting their origins to the God Who gave them. But the Satanic temptation offered to Eve, which suggests that obedience to God is to be tempered with consideration of the desirability of alternatives, is clearly echoed in the implicit endorsement here of homosexuality and heterosexual cohabitation between consenting adults without regard to the spiritual or marital implications.

The fall, in my opinion, represents the ultimate rebellion of man against God's grace in arrogant disobedience. In the process, man has lost his innate moral righteousness, his intellectual clarity, his intimate communion with the rest of God's created universe (which is also subject to the damage of the fall), and his physical health and natural immortality. Another question about the fall relates to what the Calvinist tradition has called "original sin." Two views quite opposed to each other have been held by different branches of the Reformation. Unger describes each quite succinctly in his *Bible Dictionary*:

---

21. *Manifesto II,* "The Individual."

(1) By Calvinists it has been held that the sin of Adam was immediately imputed to the whole family, so that not only is the entire race depraved, but also actually guilty on account of the first transgression. To sustain this opinion it is argued that Adam was not only the natural, but also the representative or federal head of the human race. His fall involved the whole race in guilt. . . .

(2) Arminian. The view more generally held is that the effect of Adam's sin upon the moral state of mankind is in accordance with and by virtue of the natural law of heredity. The race inherited proneness to sin. But this proneness to sin does not imply guilt, inasmuch as punishment can justly be inflicted only on account of actual sin, which consists in voluntary transgression. This view is held by many Presbyterians, Congregationalists, Episcopalians, and universally by Methodists.[22]

The position of the Disciples of Christ and the Restoration movement since the Campbells and Barton W. Stone seems somewhat blurred. Robert Richardson, Alexander Campbell's biographer, goes to great lengths to discuss the painful path which led Thomas and Alexander Campbell from infant baptism by sprinkling to the belief that believer's baptism by immersion is scriptural. Alexander's reconsideration of this question was triggered, according to Richardson, by the birth of his first child.[23] Even though the Campbells and Barton W. Stone all came from a Calvinist and Presbyterian background, it is surprising to me that Richardson did not feel called upon to explain the reformers' feelings about the primary reason for infant baptism: the belief that through original sin the child stood under condemnation until he was baptized into the grace of Christ. Later in his own life, however, Alexander Campbell spoke about original sin and articulated basically the Arminian position:

---

22. Unger, "Sin," *Op. Cit.,* p. 1028.
23. Robert Richardson, *Memoirs of Alexander Campbell* (Cincinnati: Standard Publishing Co., 1897), Chapter XVIII.

In Adam all have sinned; therefore "in Adam all die." Your nature, gentle reader, not your person, was in Adam when he put forth his hand to break the precept of Jehovah. You did not personally sin in that act; but your nature, then in the person of your father, sinned against the Author of your existence. In the just judgment, therefore, of your heavenly Father, your nature sinned in Adam, and with him it is right that all human beings should be born *mortal* and that death should lord it over the whole race as he has done in innumerable instances even "over them that have not sinned after the similitude of Adam's transgression," i.e., by violating a positive law.[24]

Campbell seems to defend with the Renaissance theologians the concept that a residue of God's image is retained by even unredeemed man after the Fall:

Still, man, with all his hereditary imbecility, is not under an invincible necessity to sin. Greatly prone to evil, easily seduced into transgression, he may or may not yield to passion and seduction. Hence the differences we so often discover in the corruption and depravity of man. All inherit a *fallen*, consequently a *sinful* nature, though all are not equally depraved. Thus we find the degrees of sinfulness and depravity are very different in different persons. And, although without a knowledge of God and his revealed will—without the interposition of a mediator and without faith in him—"it is impossible to please God," still there are those who, while destitute of this knowledge and belief, are more noble and virtuous than others. Thus admits Luke when he says, "The Jews in Berea were more noble than those in Thessalonica, in that they received the word with all readiness of mind, and searched the Scriptures daily whether these things were so."[25]

---

24. Alexander Campbell, *The Christian System* (Cincinnati: Standard Publishing Co., n.d.), pp. 14-15.
25. *Ibid.*, pp. 17-18.

THE RESTORED IMAGE OF GOD

Having suggested that all persons have been created, physically, spiritually, and intellectually in the image of God, it remains to be considered what the restored and redeemed image is like. John's Gospel states the ideal model: "And the Word became flesh and dwelt among us, full of grace and truth; we have beheld his glory, glory as of the only Son from the Father. . . . No one has ever seen God; the only Son, who is in the bosom of the Father, he has made him known."[26]

It is John also in his first New Testament letter who explains how that *Imago Dei* is restored in human beings: "No man has ever seen God; if we love one another, God abides in us and his love is perfected in us."[27]

In contradistinction, then, to all humanisms, but especially to the image of man projected by twentieth-century naturalistic humanism, what kind of person is the man or woman who has been restored by the grace of Jesus Christ to his original position of obedience and trust in his Creator—to the projected *Imago Dei*?

I should like to adopt Merrill Unger's outline here, for it seems to me the five categories he discusses describe the Biblical position concerning the Christian image of man. These categories are *spirituality, personality, holiness, love,* and *dominion.*[28]

Spirituality

Since God is a Spirit, man's likeness to God cannot be primarily in a physical sense although we do have the incarnation of His Son into a physical and human form. The eternal spirit of man, whether redeemed or unredeemed, seems to be clearly taught. Jesus made a rather unmistakable reference to eternal judgment

---

26. John 1:14, 18 (RSV).
27. I John 4:12 (RSV).
28. Unger, "Image of God," *Op. Cit.,* p. 517.

for the wicked in Mark 9:48, a passage which in turn seems to be related to the Old Testament prophet Isaiah in Chapter 66, verse 24. The dualism of body and spirit has characterized Judeo-Christian thought and thus Christian-influenced Western culture throughout the modern history of Europe, and this very dualism received a strong thrust in Lutheran doctrine in the Protestant Reformation.

The essence of a person, then, seems to be in the life originally inbreathed from God at Eden and the new life given in Christ Jesus. Man is a spiritual being. Logical positivists, who contend that the only way of knowing anything is through empirical knowledge or sense experience, behavioral psychologists who believe that the stimulus-response bond which speaks of the brain but not the mind, and naturalistic humanists are denied this vision by virtue of their monistic denial of dualism. For the Christian, however, just as God is a Spirit, man is a spiritual being. Christians believe that this is one of the most important things about *Homo sapiens* and that it is fundamental for the understanding of anything else about him.

Personality

The Christian and Biblical concept of personality denotes both individuality and intelligence. God's respect of man's individuality is suggested in the Garden of Eden when complete freedom to do good or evil was afforded to man and woman. The willingness to live as individuals and let others live their lives is one of the fundamental truths parents have to learn as their children mature and grow up. The second command, to "Love thy neighbor as thyself" commends itself to this aspect of personality. This is one of the motivating reasons why Kierkegaard broke with the Danish national church in favor of his Christian existentialism—the fact that the national church had, he felt, violated the individuality and the personal prerogatives of the individual. The refrain cultivated by Dr. Martin Luther

King and the civil rights movement, "Free at last, free at last, thank God we're free at last" is rooted squarely in the Christian doctrine of persons. "If the Son makes you free," Jesus promised, "you will be free indeed."[29] Alexander Campbell used five words to describe the freedom one receives in Christ: "Christians," he says, "are persons pardoned, justified, sanctified, adopted, saved."[30]

In thinking of the Christian image of man, one must remember that the freedom of the individual in Christ from sin, enslavement and Satan's wiles must be continually claimed. Paul's cry in the Galatian letter is militant and urgent: "For freedom Christ has set us free; stand fast therefore, and do not submit again to a yoke of slavery."[31]

Another aspect of the Christian personality is human intelligence. The Renaissance Christian humanists laid full claim to this aspect of man, sometimes to the point of pride rather than thanksgiving, but they underscored a truth which it seems may be too lightly accepted by many Christian groups in the twentieth century. If John Calvin was right, this is one mark of the *Imago Dei* which all people still carry even though human intelligence is sullied and obscured by the Fall. Twentieth-century antitheistic humanists repeatedly point to intelligence as their primary claim to the future, sometimes as though it were a humanistic invention. Unfortunately, they may have some reason to believe that many contemporary Christians have vacated this field and have apologized for their intelligence rather than sanctifying it in Christ and using it for the Kingdom of God. One may be thankful for some of the evangelical Christians who, during the past twenty or thirty years, have accepted the mental discipline necessary to study some of the hard questions and reclaim reason and intelligence in the Name of the One Who is all Wisdom and Knowledge and gave to Man whatever measure he may

29. John 8:36 (RSV).
30. Campbell, p. 46.
31. Gal. 5:1 (RSV).

have of this quality. Some of these men include people who have been quoted in this series: Barton Babbage of Australia, Os Guiness of England, H. R. Rookmaaker of the Netherlands, and Carl F. H. Henry, former Editor of *Christianity Today* in the United States.

We are inclined to be very cautious about depending on human wisdom when we read Paul's words to the Corinthians in the first letter, Chapter Two. Paul, of course, was explaining his (and no doubt the Holy Spirit's) revulsion at the arrogant intellectuality which he had met in Athens just before his first trip to Corinth. He determined that the message he presented would not depend upon human reasoning but simply upon the facts of the Gospel in Jesus Christ. This never changes. But both St. Paul and the writer of the letter to the Hebrews express deep concern about people in the church who refuse to grow in spirituality and knowledge. The Apostle John warns, "Let him who hath understanding count the number of the beast."[32]

Alexander Campbell was a child of his time just as we are children of ours. He was obviously influenced heavily by the philosophy and the methodology of rationalism, the rationalistic philosophy of John Locke and perhaps also that of Thomas Jefferson. George G. Beazley, Jr. is very frank about this heritage:

> With a powerful, logical mind, a rootage in the philosophy of John Locke, and a thorough knowledge of the Scriptures in their original tongues, Alexander Campbell constructed a systematic ecclesiology and church polity which became the official-unofficial doctrine of the Christian Church (Disciples of Christ).[33]

Campbell believed in the logical power of persuasion and debate and probably believed that the common sense of most men

---

32. Rev. 13:18b (RSV).

33. George G. Beazley, Jr., *The Christian Church (Disciples of Christ): An Interpretative Examination in the Cultural Context* (St. Louis: Bethany Press, 1973), p. 23.

and women would lead them to understand the proposition he espoused: the unity of all Christians on the basis of the Bible and the secondary proposition of restoration of the New Testament Church pattern. The generations of preachers following him, the group Beazley calls the "scholastics" of the Campbells, Scotts and Stones, became even more debate-oriented and rational in their presentation of argument, so that division, ill feeling, and radical fragmentation of the groups which emanated from the Movement resulted.

This one-sided dependence upon rational thought and its result in the history of our movement should help us appreciate Paul's reluctance to resort to "lofty words of wisdom" at Corinth. On the other hand, the challenges of truly understanding science, the humanities, contemporary political movements, and other demanding issues should not be shrugged off because we are intellectually too lazy to accept the necessary discipline to meet issues on their own ground. Man in the image of God is a rational person and God expects to be able to communicate with him through the Word, through Nature, and in turn to have his children communicate with the rest of the world.

Holiness

The letter to the church at Sardis in the Book of Revelation is strong evidence of God's expecting His people—man in His image—to be holy. The call to keep garments unsoiled and to walk with Jesus in white underlines the Old Testament admonition, "You shall be holy; for I the Lord your God am holy."[34] Any suggestion that man lives in the *Imago Dei* must include the holy and sanctified life. That holiness, of course, is imputed to man through Jesus Christ and His righteousness as Paul points out in the letter to the Romans: "Therefore, since we are justified by faith, we have peace with God through our Lord Jesus Christ."[35]

---

34. Lev. 19:2 (RSV).
35. Romans 5:1 (RSV).

Love

The word "love" stimulates numerous possible meanings in our minds and probably most of the good ones stem from our relationship to God. But the *agape* relationship, that of love which gives with no thought of receiving—as the theologians say, with no synergistic expectations like "God did His part and I will add that to my part"—this love of John 3:16 is the essence of God's Image also. John, the apostle whom Jesus loved (as John remembers it) points out the Image relationship quite logically: "God is love, and he who abides in love abides in God, and God abides in him."[36] One of the better modern-day explanations of the love which is lived in the Image of God was given by R. H. Boll:

> Now love is appreciative of others. It sees the good and the possibility of good in them. It takes account of their weakness and their trials and the struggles, whether vain or successful. It appeals to the best in them as to the true self. It beholds every man an ideal of that man, and will address itself to that ideal, in nothing put off by what the outward appearance may present to the contrary.[37]

Dominion

Dominion speaks of God's commission to man concerning the earth. Unger says:

> God is sovereign. He created man to rule (Gen. 1:26; Ps. 8:6; et al.). Whether the place assigned to man in the creation is to be considered a feature of the likeness to the divine, or, in the consequence of that likeness, is a question that has been much discussed. The latter is the more exact view, as reference is here to his position rather than to his nature. And yet man's

---

36. I John 4:16b (RSV).

37. R. H. Boll, "The Manners of Heaven," *Truth and Grace* (Cincinnati: F. L. Rowe, Publisher, 1917), pp. 97-98.

royalty in the natural world is still so great that it must suggest his original complete fitness for it.[38]

Man's restoration to that sovereign condition in the *Imago Dei* is referred to clearly in the twentieth chapter of Revelation when the martyrs of the Tribulation are called upon to reign with Christ a thousand years.[39] It seems clear to me that with the remaining evidence of God's Image in our lives, men and women are expected to exert sovereign influence over the world—perhaps the universe—now, and since "It doth not yet appear what we shall be" greater responsibility awaits us. This is a glorious chapter in the Christian image of man which is beyond compare with any wistfully-hopeful plan naturalistic humanism can offer.

John Milton caught the spirit of the incomparable Image in which man was created and redeemed in his masterpiece, *Paradise Lost*. Baron von Sweeten translated some of Milton and added his own paraphrases when he provided the libretto for Joseph Haydn's oratorio, *The Creation*. There is a tinge of Renaissance in the poem, but it still soars over the concepts of twentieth-century humanism, existentialism, behaviorism, and every other human concept of greatness in the central aria for the tenor:

> In native worth and honour clad,
> With beauty, courage, strength, adorn'd
> Erect, with front serene,
> He stands a Man, the Lord and King of nature all.
>
> His large and arched brow sublime,
> Of wisdom deep declares the seat;
> And in his eyes with brightness shines
> The soul, the breath and image of his God.[40]

---

38. Unger, "Man."
39. Rev. 20 (RSV).
40. *The Creation* (N.Y.: G. Schirmer, n.d.). Translator not included.

BIBLIOGRAPHY

Adam, James. *The Religious Teachers of Greece*. T. and T. Clark, Edinburgh, 1919.

Andrews, Elias, "Paul." *Encyclopaedia Britannica,* Vol. 17. William Benton, Publishers, Chicago, 1963.

Aquinas, Thomas. *Summa contra Gentiles* (available in various forms).

Aristotle. *Nichomachean Ethics.* translated by James E. C. Welldon, The Classics Club, New York, 1943.

Babbage, Stuart Barton. *Man in Nature and in Grace*. William B. Eerdmans Publishing Co., Grand Rapids, 1957.

Beazley, George G. Jr. *The Christian Church (Disciples of Christ): An Interpretive Examination in the Cultural Context.* Bethany Press, St. Louis, 1973.

The Holy Bible, Revised Standard Version. World Publishing Co., Cleveland and New York, 1962.

Boll, Robert H. *Truth and Grace.* F. L. Rowe, Publisher, Cincinnati, 1917.

Campbell, Alexander. *The Christian System*. Standard Publishing Company, n.d.

Chastel, Andre. *The Age of Humanism*. McGraw-Hill Book Co., Inc., 1963.

Coneybeare, W. J. and Howson, J. S. *The Life and Epistles of St. Paul.* William B. Eerdmans Publishing Co., 1980.

Coulton, G. G. *Art and the Reformation*. Anchor Books, reprinted by permission of Cambridge University Press, 1928.

Davis, M. M. *How the Disciples Began and Grew*. Standard Publishing Company, Cincinnati, 1915.

Dickens, A. G. *Reformation and Society in Sixteenth-Century Europe*. Thames and Hudson with Harcourt, Brace and Co., Inc., London, 1966.

Goines, Frank. *Prophecy and Economics*. 3:2, February 17, 1981.

Guiness, Os. *The Dust of Death*. InterVarsity Press, Downers Grove, Illinois, 1973.

Hicks, Robert D. "Stoics" in *Encyclopaedia Britannica,* Vol. 21. William Benton, Publishers, Chicago, 1963.

Hinman, Nelson E. *An Answer to Humanistic Psychology.* Harvest House Publishers, Irvine, California, 1980.

Homer. *The Iliad.* translated by Samuel Butler, The Classics Club, New York, 1942.

Ingersoll, Robert G. quoted in Morley, Christopher, Editor, *Familiar Quotations.* Little Brown and Co., Boston, 1937.

Kierkegaard, Søren. *The Sickness unto Death.* translated by Walter Lowrie, Princeton University Press, Princeton, N.J., 1941.

Kouwenhoven, John A. *The Arts in Modern American Civilization.* W. W. Norton Co., Inc., New York, 1948.

Kurtz, Paul. *The Humanist Alternative.* Prometheus Books, Buffalo, New York, 1973.

Lamont, Corliss. *The Philosophy of Humanism.* 5th Edition, Frederick Unger Publishing Co., New York, 1949 (1977).

Loomis, Louise. "Introduction" to *The Iliad of Homer.* translated by Samuel Butler, The Classics Club, New York, 1942.

Maritain, Jacques. *Integral Humanism.* University of Notre Dame Press, South Bend, Indiana, 1973.

Mayer, Frederic. *A History of Modern Philosophy.* American Book Co., New York, 1951.

Morain, Lloyd. "Humanist Manifesto II—A Time for Reconsideration?" *The Humanist,* Sept./Oct., 1980.

O'Kelly, Bernard, Ed. *The Renaissance Image of Man and the World.* Ohio State University Press, Columbus, 1966.

Richardson, Robert. *Memoirs of Alexander Campbell.* Standard Publishing Company, Cincinnati, 1897.

Riesman, David. *The Lonely Crowd.* Yale University Press, New Haven, 1973.

Rookmaaker, H. R. *Modern Art and the Death of a Culture.* InterVarsity Press, Downers Grove, Illinois, 1970.

Sartre, Jean Paul. *Existentialism and Humanism.* translated by Philip Mairet, Haskell House Publishers, Ltd., Brooklyn, 1977.

Speer, Albert. *Infiltration*. Macmillan Publishing Company, New York, 1981.

Spinka, Matthew. *Christian Thought from Erasmus to Berdyaev*. Prentice-Hall, Inc., Englewood Cliffs, N.J., 1962.

Symonds, J. A. "Renaissance." *Encyclopaedia Britannica*, Vol. 19, William Benton, Publishers, Chicago, 1963.

Taylor, Edwin F. "The Limits of Scientific Knowledge." *The Christian Scholar* XLIII/2, Summer, 1960.

Unger, Merrill F. "Image of God," "Sin" and "The Fall" in *Unger's Bible Dictionary*, Moody Press, Chicago, 1957.

Warnock, Robert and Anderson, George, Editors. *The World in Literature*. Scott, Foresman and Company, Chicago, 1950 (1959).

White, William Luther. *The Image of Man in C. S. Lewis*. Abingdon Press, Nashville and New York, 1969.

Wilburn, Ralph G. "Disciple Thought in Protestant Perspective: An Interpretation," in Ralph Wilburn (Ed.), *The Reconstruction of Theology*. Bethany Press, St. Louis, 1963.

Zimmerman, Karl. *Der Apostel Paulus, ein Lebensbild*. Zwingli Verlag, Zurich, 1962.